ISBN 978-0-428-59788-7
PIBN 11247535

This book is a reproduction of an important historical work. Forgotten Books uses state-of-the-art technology to digitally reconstruct the work, preserving the original format whilst repairing imperfections present in the aged copy. In rare cases, an imperfection in the original, such as a blemish or missing page, may be replicated in our edition. We do, however, repair the vast majority of imperfections successfully; any imperfections that remain are intentionally left to preserve the state of such historical works.

Historic, archived document

Do not assume content reflects current
scientific knowledge, policies, or practices.

Agricultural

Economics

Research

APRIL 1965   Vol. XVII, No. 2

---

in this issue

UNITED STATES DEPARTMENT OF AGRICULTURE   ●   Economic Res

CONTRIBUTORS

J. DAWSON AHALT is an Agricultural Econo-
mist with the Economic and Statistical Analysis
Division, ERS. ALVIN C. EGBERT is Head of
the Long-run Projections Section, Outlook and
Projections Branch, Economic and Statistical
Analysis Division, ERS.

GEORGE A. PAVELIS is Leader of Water Use
Investigations in the Land and Water Branch,
Resource Development Economics Division,
ERS.

SHERMAN E. JOHNSON is Deputy Adminis-
trator for Foreign Economics, ERS.

QUENTIN M. WEST is Deputy Director, Foreign
Regional Analysis Division, ERS.

REX F. DALY, Chief, Outlook and Projections
Branch, Economic and Statistical Analysis Division, ERS, spent several weeks in Mexico in
spring 1965 as consultant to the Development
and Trade Analysis Division, ERS.

MARSHALL H. COHEN is an Economist in the
Outlook and Projections Branch, Economic and
Statistical Analysis Division, ERS.

MARTIN KRIESBERG, Office of the Adminis-
trator, International Agricultural Development
Service, has been on several overseas assign-
ments for the Ford Foundation, United Nations,
and USDA-AID.

H. ALBERT GREEN is Leader of Area Structure
and Economic Growth Investigations, Area Economic Development Branch, ERS.

ALAN R. BIRD is Leader of Rural Renewal
and Development Investigations, Resource Development Economics Division, ERS. He evaluates public programs that aid rural development and contribute to the war on poverty.

HOWARD L. HALL, Agricultural Economist,
Foreign Regional Analysis Division, ERS, is
Assistant Chief of the Western Hemisphere
Branch with current responsibility for work
on Canadian problems.

VIVIAN WISER, Agricultural Historian with the
Economic and Statistical Analysis Division,
ERS, is currently working on a history of per-
sonnel administration in the USDA.

Agricultural

Economics

Research

*A Journal of Economic and Statistical Research
in the United States Department of Agriculture
and Cooperating Agencies.*

APRIL 1965 — Vol. XVII, No. 2

Editors
  Elizabeth Lane
  Rex F. Daly
Book Review Editor
  Wayne D. Rasmussen
Assistant Editors
  Kenneth E. Ogren
  Ronald L. Mighell
  Raymond P. Christensen
  Bruce W. Kelly

The Demand for Feed Concentrates:
A Statistical Analysis

By J. Dawson Ahalt and Alvin C. Egbert

THE STATISTICAL demand functions presented in this paper were designed to complement recursive livestock supply-demand models, and to provide a basis for appraising feed consumption under alternative programs and for projecting the demand for feed.[1] Although a number of statistical analyses of the demand for feed have been made (2, 5, 6, 7, 8, 12),[2] none of these were oriented toward policy analysis or toward the Department's long-run projections work.

This analysis considers only highly aggregated data. No attempt is made, for example, to estimate the demand for feed by kinds of livestock, nor the demand for specific feeds. Some general questions which such aggregative analyses can help to answer are:

(1) What is the effect of a change in feed or livestock prices on the quantity of concentrates fed?

(2) What will be the effect on total demand for feed of a change in total livestock output or a change in the livestock product mix?

(3) With unrestricted production, at what price would supply and demand for feed be in balance?

Major Conclusions

The great increase in concentrate feeding in the postwar years, and particularly in the last decade, can be largely explained by economic factors. Although technological developments are changing feed conversion rates, the actual level of feeding depends heavily on the economic forces facing the livestock producer. Changes in livestock production (measured by livestock

production units)[3] and in prices of concentrates relative to prices of livestock products explain most of the annual variation as well as the uptrend in concentrate feeding during the last decade.

The analyses indicate that a 10 percent increase in livestock production units during postwar years was associated with an average increase of about 13 percent in total concentrates fed, and also in feed grains fed, while use of high-protein feeds increased about 20 percent.

The analyses also indicate that total concentrate consumption rises as the product-feed price ratio improves. A 10 percent increase in this ratio in the postwar years, with livestock production units constant, was accompanied by an increase of about 2-1/2 percent in total concentrate use. Because product prices and feed prices enter into the statistical demand function as a ratio, the elasticity of feed use with respect to livestock price is the same as for feed prices but with opposite algebraic sign. Thus a 10 percent increase in product prices has the same effect on output as a 10 percent decrease in the price of feed.

Demand relations for feed are useful in conjunction with a livestock model to assess the effects of changing feed prices on livestock production, quantity of feed used, and feed consumption rates. In an illustrative example, a decrease in the price of corn of about 30 percent resulted in a 14 percent increase in total concentrates used. This total increase was the product of a 5 percent increase in livestock production units and an 8 percent increase in the feeding rate. Livestock prices declined with the increased livestock output that resulted from lower feed prices, but

---

[1] The authors wish to thank Rex F. Daly and Shlomo Reutlinger for many comments and suggestions that have helped to improve this paper.

[2] Underscored numbers in parentheses refer to Literature Cited, p. 49.

[3] The livestock production unit is the sum of all livestock production weighted by feeding rates in some base period (9).

relatively less than feed prices. This improvement in the product-feed price ratio accounted for part of the rise in the feeding rate.

Postwar Developments in the Feed-Livestock Sector

Total concentrates fed to livestock rose sharply in the postwar period. They increased from 103.7 million tons in 1947-48 to 152.0 million in 1962-63, or nearly 47 percent. The use of high-protein concentrate feeds increased 75 percent, from 10.2 million to 17.9 million tons, during the same period. Consumption of feed grains increased 53 percent, rising from 78.9 million tons in 1947-48 to 120.8 million tons in 1962-63.

Livestock output increased about 30 percent from 1947-48 to 1962-63. Livestock production units--a measure of feed requirements--increased 28 percent in the same period. This increase in livestock production accounted for much of the increase in concentrate use, but higher rates of feeding also contributed.

In standard feed units, which weight all feeds by their nutritive value in terms of corn, feed consumed per livestock production unit rose from 0.690 ton in 1947-48 to 0.787 in 1962-63, an increase of 14 percent ($\underline{9}, \underline{10}, \underline{11}$). Actual weight of feed fed per livestock production unit rose from 0.634 ton in 1947-48 to 0.723 ton in 1962-63, also an increase of 14 percent. The difference in the absolute values of these feeding rates is due to the heavier feeding value assigned to high-protein concentrates in calculating the standard feed unit. We used the widely published actual weight as a basis for analysis, as the year-to-year changes in these two series are about proportional.

Major factors responsible for the increase in concentrate feeding since World War II appear to be:

(1) Improvement in livestock prices relative to feed prices which has encouraged a general expansion in the livestock industry;

(2) More favorable product-feed price relationships which have enabled some individual livestock enterprises to step up the rate of feeding;

(3) Changing composition of livestock and livestock product output;

(4) Technological improvements in poultry production which have brought about multiple increases in broiler and turkey output;

(5) Changes in composition of feeds fed.

During the postwar period, average prices of livestock and livestock products have moved downward, although varying widely primarily because of livestock production cycles. The price index for all livestock declined nearly 12 percent from 1947 to 1962. However, the livestock-feed price ratio increased about 48 percent, as feed prices declined more than livestock prices. Feed grain prices have been under support programs throughout the postwar period. Technological developments in grain production have resulted in rapidly mounting Government stocks, as production increased more rapidly than domestic and foreign markets under existing support prices. With mounting pressure of stocks, price supports were lowered in the latter part of the 1950's. As price supports were lowered, market prices of feed also declined, falling about 40 percent from 1947 to 1962 (fig. 1).

The overall improvement in product-feed price relationships has had both short- and long-run effects on feed use. In the short run, producers have tended to respond to more favorable prices by feeding their existing livestock at higher rates. In the long run, favorable livestock-feed price ratios can result in increased investment in livestock enterprises and expanding output (fig. 2). During 1947-62, moreover, there were two significant changes in the

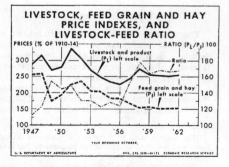

Figure 1

42

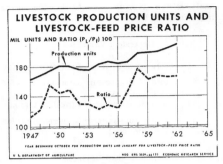

LIVESTOCK PRODUCTION UNITS AND
LIVESTOCK-FEED PRICE RATIO

Figure 2

livestock industry which affect feed consumption: changes in the output mix and changes in feeding efficiency. Broiler production increased more than sixfold from 1947 to 1962. During the same period, turkey production more than doubled. Fed beef rose from 34 percent of all beef produced in 1947 to 57 percent in 1960 (3). These increases in poultry and fed beef production had somewhat offsetting effects on the average feeding rate for all livestock. According to available data, broilers currently consume about 2-1/2 pounds of concentrates per pound of product. Fed beef consume over 5 pounds of concentrates per pound of beef added in the feed lot. However, some evidence indicates that this feeding rate for beef may be too low (2).

Significant changes have occurred in livestock production technology in the last two decades. Feeding efficiency in broiler production increased from 26 percent in 1947 to 40 percent in 1962.[4] Without this advance in efficiency, total feed requirements would have been much greater today. On the other hand, feeding efficiency in dairy production apparently has declined as milk production per cow has been pushed to higher levels. Although the quality of dairy cows has improved, higher milk production per cow has been attained mainly by higher feeding rates per cow. From 1947 to 1962, milk production per cow increased 47 percent. Concentrates fed per cow increased about 80 per-

_____
[4]Here we define feeding efficiency as pounds of output per pound of concentrates fed.

cent and concentrates fed per 100 pounds of milk produced increased about 20 percent in the same period.

Changes in the individual product-feed price ratios appear to explain the increased production of grain-fattened beef and higher output per dairy cow (fig. 3). The beef steer-corn price ratio increased almost 90 percent from 1947 to 1962 while the milk-feed price ratio increased nearly 20 percent.

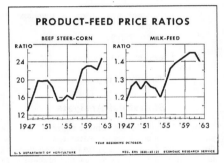

PRODUCT-FEED PRICE RATIOS

Figure 3

Demand for Feed Concentrates

The demand for feed--a factor of production rather than a final good--is derived from, or a function of, the demand for livestock and livestock products. But in another sense, feed demand is a function of the supply of animal products--supply which depends on current production technology, product and factor prices, and other variables. The amount of feed used in any period is the result of all the forces underlying supply and demand for feed-using final products.

The static theory of demand for factors of production under perfect competition is well developed (1, pp. 369-374; 8, ch. 3). However, we need to estimate the demand for feed in its actual dynamic setting. For the analysis reported here, we were guided by economic and statistical theory as well as our practical needs for estimates of feed use that could be integrated

43

with a long-run livestock model. In the relatively simple dynamic analysis which follows, we assume that expected prices are simple functions of past prices and that livestock production units are a relevant demand shifter. The general demand function is as follows:

(1) $F_t = f(L_t, P_{L_{t-i}}, P_{f_{t-i}}, u_t)$

where:

F_t = feed use in year t.

L_t = livestock production or inventory in year t.

$P_{L_{t-i}}$ = livestock prices in year t-i.

$P_{f_{t-i}}$ = feed prices in year t-i.

u_t = disturbance in year t.

Statistical Analysis

Several multiple and simple regression analyses were made to obtain estimates of the total demand for feed concentrates and the demand for such major groups as low and high-protein concentrates and feed grains. Least-squares regressions, in linear and logarithmic form, were fitted to the following variables for feeding years 1947-48 to 1962-63. Data used in the

analyses are given in table 1. (Feeding years begin October 1.)

Dependent Variables

F_c = total concentrates fed (million tons).

F_{Lp} = total low-protein concentrates fed (million tons).

F_g = total feed grains fed (million tons).

F_{hp} = total high-protein concentrates fed (million tons).

Independent Variables

L_{pu} = total livestock production units (millions).

A_u = total grain-consuming animal units (millions).

H_{pu} = total high-protein animal units (millions).

P_L = index of livestock and livestock product prices received by farmers, 1910-14 = 100, calendar year.

P_f = index of feed grain and hay prices received by farmers, 1910-14 = 100, calendar year.

P_L/P_f = ratio of livestock and product prices to feed grains and hay prices, multiplied by 100.

T = trend, 1947-48 = 1.

Table 1.--Statistical data used in the analysis

Year beginning October 1	Total concentrates fed (F_c)	Feed grains fed (F_g)	Low-protein concentrates fed (F_{Lp})	High-protein concentrates fed (F_{hp})	Livestock production units (L_{pu})	Grain consuming animal units (A_u)	High-protein animal units (H_{pu})	Livestock product prices (P_L) 1910-14 = 100	Feed grain and hay prices (P_f) 1910-14=100	Livestock-feed price ratio (P_L/P_f) 1910-14= 100	Feed concentrates fed per L_{pu} (F_c/L_{pu})
	Mil. tons	Mil. tons	Mil. tons	Mil.tons	Million	Million	Million	Index	Index	Index	Tons
1947......	103.7	78.9	93.5	10.2	163.6	153.1	126.5	288	256	113	0.634
1948......	111.7	88.6	100.4	11.3	168.4	158.6	130.9	315	258	122	.663
1949......	118.3	94.1	106.3	12.0	175.3	163.8	134.2	272	177	154	.675
1950......	121.7	96.2	108.4	13.3	181.5	168.1	136.4	280	193	145	.671
1951......	124.1	98.0	110.7	13.4	181.1	167.3	137.0	336	226	149	.685
1952......	114.0	88.0	100.9	13.1	176.4	158.9	133.8	306	234	131	.646
1953......	116.6	90.7	103.3	13.3	174.7	156.9	133.5	268	206	130	.667
1954......	116.2	90.9	103.1	13.1	183.4	161.6	135.0	249	203	123	.634
1955......	121.9	95.9	107.8	14.1	187.7	165.3	138.4	234	183	128	.649
1956......	119.7	93.6	105.1	14.6	184.1	160.9	136.6	226	182	124	.650
1957......	129.0	101.5	113.8	15.2	186.5	159.9	135.8	244	166	147	.692
1958......	139.5	110.7	123.0	16.5	198.2	167.7	140.8	273	154	177	.704
1959......	144.7	115.8	128.7	16.0	198.7	165.7	139.6	256	156	164	.728
1960......	150.3	120.6	133.5	16.8	202.7	167.6	143.0	253	151	168	.741
1961......	152.9	122.2	135.4	17.5	204.7	169.0	143.4	251	151	166	.747
1962......	152.0	120.8	134.1	17.9	210.1	172.5	146.5	255	153	167	.723

Source: (14, 15).

44

Table 2 shows the standard regression statistics derived. Elasticities computed at the mean values of the variables are also included. Equations (1.1) and (1.2) estimate the demand for total feed concentrates. These equations follow the general hypothesis stated in equation (1). Both equations account for 96 percent of the total variation in the consumption of feed concentrates over the period. Equation (1.1) predicts feed utilization rather well. Estimated values for total concentrates used, based on equation (1.1), are plotted beside the actual feed used from 1947-48 to 1962-63 in figure 4. In terms of turning points, this equation predicts in the correct direction except for three seasons--1953-54, 1959-60, and 1962-63. However, in 1958-59, the estimated value exceeded the actual value of total concentrate use by 5.9 million tons. This overestimate causes the predicted value of 1959-60 to appear to move in the wrong direction. Equation (1.2) gives comparable results for the analysis period, but because it involves logarithms, it is more cumbersome to use than equation (1.1).

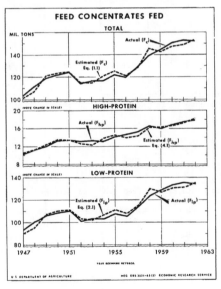

Figure 4

For linear relationships, the elasticity varies at each point on the demand curve. For equation (1.1), the elasticity computed at the mean for feed consumption is 1.28 with respect to livestock production units, 0.25 with respect to price of livestock, and -0.25 with respect to feed grain and hay prices. Evaluation of the variables at 1959-61 levels yields elasticities of 1.19 with respect to L_{pu} and 0.26 with respect to the livestock-feed price ratio. For equations which are linear in logarithmic form, such as equation (1.2), the elasticity is the same at each point on the curve and equals the regression coefficient derived for each variable. Equation (1.2) has an elasticity of feed use relative to L_{pu} of 1.23; that for the product-feed price ratio is 0.26.

Equations (1.1) through (3.1) assume that producers respond to relative livestock-feed prices rather than absolute prices. If this is true, product and factor price elasticities are equal. Some studies of the demand for feed grains used livestock and feed prices as separate independent variables. These analyses resulted in higher elasticities for livestock prices than for feed prices, as might be expected ([5, 6, 7]). King ([12]) specified prices of high-protein feed, corn, and livestock as separate independent variables in estimating the demand for feed grains used for feed. In contrast, his analysis yielded a higher absolute elasticity for corn than for livestock prices. This does not seem logical as feed costs are only a part of total costs. The decision to use price ratios in this analysis was based on theoretical considerations as well as exploratory empirical analysis. In two exploratory analyses, the price of feed was specified as a separate independent variable, but the price coefficient was nonsignificant.

In all analyses where livestock-production units were used as an explanatory variable, the elasticity of feed use relative to L_{pu} was greater than one. For example, in equation (1.1), a 1 percent increase in livestock production units was associated with an increase of about 1.3 percent in feed concentrate consumption. When the elasticity of feed consumption with respect to livestock production units is greater than one, the feeding rate increases as livestock production units rise. A similar result was obtained for grain-consuming animal units ([5]).

45

Table 2.--Regression coefficients of demand equations for total concentrates, low-protein feeds, feed grains, and high-protein feeds [1] [2]

Equation	Dependent variable	L_{pu}	A_u	H_{pu}	[3] P_L/P_f	T	Constant	R^2
(1.1)....	F_c	0.878 (.115) [1.28]			0.233 (.075) [.25]		-68.053	.96
(1.2)[4]...	F_c'	1.231 (.152)			0.264 (.076)		-1.259	.96
(1.3)....	F_c		0.806 (.599) [1.04]		0.519 (.157) [.58]		-79.466	.81
(2.1)....	F_{Lp}	0.713 (.114) [1.17]			0.233 (.074) [.28]		-51.556	.95
(3.1)....	F_g	0.720 (.103) [1.33]			0.215 (.067) [.30]		-64.470	.96
(4.1)....	F_{hp}	0.165 (.010) [2.15]					-16.493	[5] .95
(4.2)....	F_{hp}			0.425 (.037) [4.08]			-43.956	[5] .90
(4.3)....	F_{hp}					0.454 (.029) [6] [0.03]	10.402	[5] .95

[1] Estimated by least squares. Standard errors are shown in parentheses and elasticities computed at the mean are shown in brackets.

[2] F_c = total concentrates fed
F_{Lp} = total low-protein concentrates fed
F_g = total feed grains fed
F_{hp} = total high-protein concentrates fed
L_{pu} = total livestock production units
A_u = total grain-consuming animal units
H_{pu} = total high-protein-consuming animal units
P_L/P_f = ratio of livestock and livestock product prices to feed grain and hay prices
T = trend

[3] Elasticities are shown with respect to price of livestock and livestock products. Use of a price ratio implies the same absolute value but a negative sign with respect to feed grain and hay prices.

[4] This is a linear equation in logarithms.

[5] Simple correlation coefficient (r^2).

[6] Time elasticity formula:

$$\frac{\dot{F}_{hp}}{F_{hp}} \quad \text{where} \quad \dot{F}_{hp} = \frac{d\,F_{hp}}{d\,T}$$

Livestock production units appear to be a better estimator for shifts in feed demand than grain-consuming animal units (9).[5] The relationship based on animal units, equation (1.3), explained only 81 percent of the total variation in feed concentrates fed.[6] Moreover, the regression coefficient of the grain-consuming animal units variable has such a large standard error that it is not significantly different from zero at the 10 percent probability level.

Elasticities, however, derived at the mean for equation (1.3) appear logical. The elasticity of concentrate consumption with respect to A_u is 1.04 and the elasticity relative to the product-feed price ratio is 0.58. Compared with equations (1.1) and (1.2), this analysis gives an elasticity smaller in value with respect to the livestock variable and higher in value with respect to relative prices. Part of this difference in magnitude is explained by lower correlation between grain-consuming animal units and feed concentrate consumption.

Equation (2.1) estimates the demand for low-protein concentrates for feed. Low-protein concentrates in this analysis include the four feed grains (corn, oats, barley, and grain sorghum), wheat and rye, and low-protein byproduct feeds such as flour mill feeds. This analysis explained 95 percent of the total variation in low-protein feed consumed over the period analyzed. All coefficients are statistically significant at the 1 percent probability level. Accordingly, predicted values of this equation follow closely the actual values (fig. 4). Elasticities calculated at the mean for equation (2.1) imply that a 1 percent increase in L_{pu} was associated with a 1.17 percent increase in the consumption of low-protein concentrates, and a 1 percent improvement in the product-price ratio increased consumption by 0.28 percent.

Equation (3.1) estimates the demand for the four feed grains only. This analysis also shows a high correlation as well as logical and statistically significant coefficients. Since we expect substitution to take place in the live-stock rations when relative feed prices change, use of separate functions for low proteins, high proteins, and the feed grains may give more accurate results than functions for all concentrates, such as (1.1). Elasticities from table 2 show, on the average, that a 1 percent increase in the number of livestock-production units will increase feed grains fed by 1.33 percent. A 1 percent improvement in livestock prices will increase consumption by 0.30 percent, and a 1 percent reduction in feed grain and hay prices will also increase consumption by 0.30 percent.

In this analysis, high-protein feeds include total oilseed cake and meal, animal protein, and the high-protein grain byproduct feeds. By definition, high-protein concentrates fed plus the low-protein feed concentrates equal total concentrates fed. A comprehensive study of high-protein feed demand was published by King in 1958 (12). The simple analysis presented here deals with a more recent period and the form of the equation is compatible with our general framework for projections.

Several analyses were made to estimate high-protein feed use based on prices of all high-protein feeds, feed grain prices, and other price ratios. However, these analyses were excluded from the paper because of nonsignificant variables and poor predictability.[7] Part of the difficulty in obtaining significant price-quantity relationships for high-protein feeds is due to the ever increasing use of this concentrate. Substantial increases in demand due to unidentified factors have tended to overshadow much of the price influence in recent years.

Technological advances in formula feeding in the postwar period have been sizable (11, 13). Specialized feeds or formula rations, which increased more than 13 percent from 1954 and 1958, are using increasing amounts of high-protein feeds (15). If better managed, larger scale feeding operations based on formula feeds become more prevalent, we may expect high-protein feeds to be used more in line with maximum economic efficiency.

Equation (4.1), which uses livestock-production units (L_{pu}) as a demand shifter, gave

---

[5] A similar formulation using livestock production instead of production units (4) reports an elasticity of feed use relative to output of 1.0 and 4.5 for feed use relative to the product-feed price ratio. These relationships were approximated on the basis of changes in the past decade.

[6] Animal units were used as a demand shifter in (5), (6), and (7).

[7] Readers interested in seeing the equations may obtain them from the authors.

somewhat better results than an analysis based on high-protein animal units (H_{pu}), equation (4.2). During the period of analysis, L_{pu} increased at a more rapid rate than the high-protein animal units. Equation (4.3) shows the strong trend ($r^2 = .95$) present in the disappearance of high-protein concentrates (F_{hp}).

The center section of figure 4 compares the predicted values from equation (4.1) with the actual consumption of high-protein feeds. Table 1 also gives the elasticities for the single-variable high-protein equations. On the average, a 1 percent increase in L_{pu} implies a 2.15 percent increase in high-protein feed consumption. The elasticity of high-protein feed fed with respect to the number of protein-consuming animal units (H_{pu}) is 4.08, evaluated at the mean. For the trend equation (4.3) the elasticity shown in table 2 is a time elasticity and is not computed at the mean value.

When the demand for feed concentrates is estimated separately using equations (2.1) and (4.1), the sum of these estimates is about the same as the single aggregate estimate of total concentrate consumption using equation (1.1). The R^2 for the sum of the individual estimates is 0.96. In this sense, the individual estimates are consistent.

A Hypothetical Application

Analyses of the demand for feed can be used as a basis for estimating feed utilization at various levels of livestock production, given prices for feed grains and livestock products. Moreover, demand analyses for feed as presented here can be used in connection with demand and supply response frameworks for the livestock sector of the economy. In these, either the price or the supply of feed grains is given and livestock production and prices are generated by supply response and demand functions.

To illustrate, we estimate livestock production units, livestock prices, and feed consumption on the basis of an integrated livestock model, given the price of corn, technological developments, population, and income growth.[8] Total livestock production units, with corn at 75 cents a bushel, are estimated to be about 5-1/2 percent larger than with corn at $1.10 per bushel (table 3). Prices of livestock products are about 10 percent lower and the livestock-feed price ratio is nearly one-third higher for

[8] The model we used was developed by Shlomo Reutlinger and others.

Table 3.--Estimated livestock production, feed concentrate use, and feeding rate associated with alternative corn prices

Item	Variable	Unit	Corn price		Percentage change in variable when corn price changes from $1.10 to $0.75
			$1.10	$0.75	
Livestock production units..	L_{pu}	Mil. units	203.0	214.0	5.4
Livestock price index.......	P_L	(1910-14=100)	223	200	-10.3
Feed grain & hay price index	P_f	do.	164	111	-32.3
Livestock-feed price ratio..	P_L/P_f	--	136	180	32.4
Feed concentrate use:					
Total concentrates........	F_c	Mil. tons	140.5	160.0	13.9
Low-protein concentrates..	F_{Lp}	do.	123.5	141.2	14.3
Feed grains..............	F_g	do.	110.9	128.3	15.7
High proteins............	F_{hp}	do.	17.0	18.8	10.6
Aggregate feeding rate......	F_c/L_{pu}	--	.692	.748	8.1

75-cent corn than for $1.10 corn. With these same relationships, feed concentrate use is estimated about 14 percent larger with corn at 75 cents a bushel; low-protein concentrate use is 14 percent larger, feed grain use is nearly 16 percent larger, high-protein feed use is about 11 percent larger, and the overall feeding rate per livestock production unit is about 8 percent higher with corn at 75 cents than at $1.10 a bushel.

Although greatly oversimplified, the above illustrates the relationships, types of information used and generated, and the approximate magnitude of relationships among livestock production, feed and livestock prices, and feed utilization. Estimated feed consumption, the major end use of feed grains, provides a basis for estimating production, as well as acreage and other resources committed for feed production.

Literature Cited

(1) Allen, R. G. D. Mathematical analysis for economists. MacMillan and Co., Ltd., London, 548 pp., 1956.

(2) Brandow, G. E. Interrelations among demands for farm products and implications for control of market supply. Pa. Agr. Expt. Sta. Bul. 680, University Park, 124 pp., August 1961.

(3) Breimyer, H. F. Demand and prices for meat. U.S. Dept. Agr., Tech. Bul. 1253, 108 pp., December 1961.

(4) Daly, R. F. Agriculture in the years ahead. Paper presented at meeting of Agr. Econ. and Rural Sociol. Sec., Assoc. Southern Agr. Workers, Atlanta, Ga. U.S. Dept. Agr., 26 pp., February 1964.

(5) Foote, R. J. Statistical analyses relating to the feed-livestock economy. U.S. Dept. Agr., Tech. Bul. 1070, 41 pp., June 1953.

(6) Foote, R. J., J. W. Klein, and M. Clough. The demand and price structure for corn and total feed concentrates. U.S. Dept. Agr., Tech. Bul. 1061, 79 pp., October 1952.

(7) Hee, Olman. Analysis of selected factors affecting the quantity of corn and total feed grains consumed by livestock. U.S. Dept. Agr., Feed Situation, Fds-195, pp. 21-27, September 1962.

(8) Heady, E. O., and L. G. Tweeten. Resource demand and structure of the agricultural industry. Iowa State Univ. Press, Ames, 515 pp., 1962.

(9) Hodges, E. F. Livestock-feed relationships 1909-1963. U.S. Dept. Agr., Statis. Bul. 337, 49 pp., November 1963.

(10) Hodges, E. F. Consumption of feed by livestock 1940-59. U.S. Dept. Agr., Prod. Res. Rpt. 79, 94 pp., March 1964.

(11) Jennings, R. D. Consumption of feed by livestock 1909-56. U.S. Dept. Agr., Prod. Res. Rpt. 21, 128 pp., November 1958.

(12) King, G. A. The demand and price structure for byproduct feeds. U.S. Dept. Agr., Tech. Bul. 1183, 158 pp., August 1958.

(13) Mighell, R. L., and O. J. Scoville. Economic effects of progress in animal feeding. Agr. Econ. Res., Vol. 8, No. 3, pp. 119-127, October 1956.

(14) U.S. Department of Agriculture. Agricultural prices--1963 annual summary. Statis. Rptg. Serv., Crop Rptg. Bd., 182 pp., June 1964.

(15) U.S. Department of Agriculture. Grain and feed statistics through 1961. Statis. Bul. 159, 114 pp., rev. June 1962. Supplement for 1963, 65 pp., March 1964.

Irrigation Policy and Long-Term Growth Functions

By George A. Pavelis

A method for projecting the acreage of farmland irrigated in the 22 major water resource regions of the United States is described in this paper.[1] The method incorporates: (1) A statistical analysis of historical rates of irrigation development observed between 1939 and 1959 in the Census of Agriculture; (2) economic limits on irrigation that recognize regional variations in soils and water supplies; and (3) estimates of the absolute and relative importance (in terms of acreage) of new Federal and non-Federal irrigation development. The method is then used to quantify regional variations in the sensitivity of irrigation to three postulated irrigation policies, ranging from one involving minimal Federal and modest non-Federal development to one postulating no policy constraints on either type of development.

Background and Concepts

Figure 1 shows the distribution of the 33 million acres or so of irrigation reported for the United States in the 1959 Census of Agriculture (2).[2] About 141,000 acres were reported for Hawaii in 1959 and only 360 acres for Alaska. Figure 2 shows approximate national

totals for the last five Censuses, as well as the acreage irrigated from streams, reservoirs, or other surface sources compared with the acreage supplied from wells. About 20 percent of the gross value of all crops in 1959 was attributed to irrigation--practiced on about 8.5 percent of the total acreage of harvested crops and on about 7.4 percent of all land then classed as usable for crop production. As shown in figure 3, these percentages vary widely among States and regions. Additional details on regional characteristics of irrigation are available elsewhere, notably in official Census reports (2) and in a Department of Agriculture report by Wooten, Gertel, and Pendleton (10). A straightforward extrapolation of 1939-59 regional trends indicates that a total of about 38.7 million acres of irrigated land in farms might be reported in the Census for 1964. Preliminary county and State returns are scheduled for release beginning in April 1965.

Concerning the future, a number of completed research studies have been addressed to the problem of projecting irrigation's general role in agricultural production, and also its special importance in regional patterns of water supply and demand (4, 5, 6, 8, 9). In pointing up the sensitivity of projections of regional water demands to technologic and economic assumptions concerning irrigation, the studies have all shown a major concern with the relatively indefinite future, but somewhat less concern with irrigation policy as it relates to achieving the levels of farm output calculated as being needed at specified dates. Given various hypotheses of the extent to which additional private or public development might be encouraged by policymakers, this paper develops corresponding continuous hypothetical growth functions, enabling one not only to estimate the time path of irrigation as conditioned by specified policies, but also to identify policy constraints consistent with acreages of irrigated land computed as being optimal for specified dates.

[1] Summarized from an unpublished report presented in the Natural Resources session of the joint 1964 meeting of the Operations Research Society of America and The Institute of Management Science, Minneapolis, Minn., October 7-9, 1964. The research described is underway in collaboration with the Economic Research Service in a North Central Region cooperative project (NC-57) on "Economic and Legal Factors in Providing, Using, and Managing Water Resources in Agriculture," and in a Western Region project (W-81) on "The Economics of Water Transfer: an Appraisal of Institutions." The author appreciates the comments and suggestions of Emery N. Castle, Harold H. Ellis, Karl Gertel, Robert C. Otte, and Gordon D. Rose. Also appreciated is the assistance of Jeremiah R. Williams in the statistical phases of the study reported.

[2] Underlined numbers in parentheses refer to Literature Cited, p. 60.

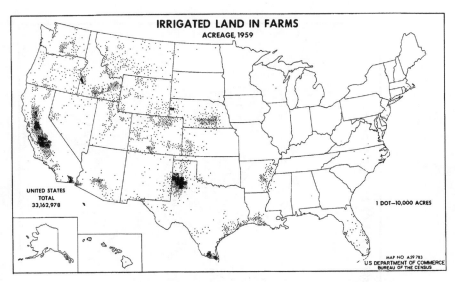

IRRIGATED LAND IN FARMS
ACREAGE, 1959

UNITED STATES
TOTAL
33,162,978

1 DOT—10,000 ACRES

MAP NO. A59 783
US DEPARTMENT OF COMMERCE
BUREAU OF THE CENSUS

Figure 1

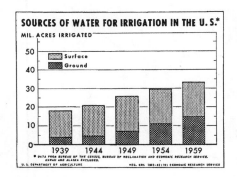

SOURCES OF WATER FOR IRRIGATION IN THE U. S.*

MIL. ACRES IRRIGATED

Surface
Ground

1939 1944 1949 1954 1959

* DATA FROM BUREAU OF THE CENSUS, BUREAU OF RECLAMATION AND ECONOMIC RESEARCH SERVICE.
HAWAII AND ALASKA EXCLUDED.

U. S. DEPARTMENT OF AGRICULTURE   NEG. ERS 1382-62 (10) ECONOMIC RESEARCH SERVICE

Figure 2

General Method

First, a maximum economic limit on the acreage of land irrigable in the indefinite future is postulated for each of the 22 regions in figure 3. Second, the present acreage is specified as a benchmark, and the difference between it and the maximum limit is considered to be the maximum remaining potential increase in each region. The present acreage is taken as the trend value for 1959, the most recent year of completely published observations. It is further assumed that the maximum potential increase will never accrue fully for any region; this means that acreages in the indefinite future will become asymptotic to the maximum initially specified. A final "premise" involves the selection of equation types thought best for combining information on the defined limits to irrigation, the acreage recorded to the present, historical rates of change, and anticipated rates of change.

Policy constraints are introduced simply by reducing maximum remaining potentials in

51

52

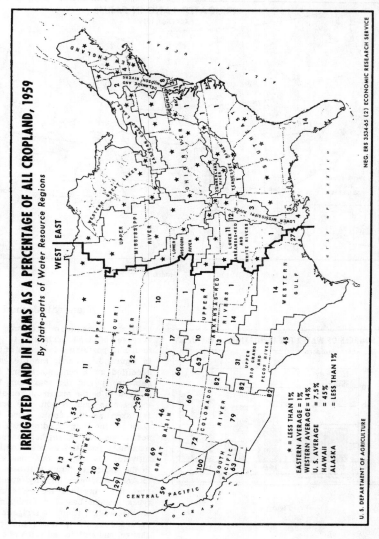

IRRIGATED LAND IN FARMS AS A PERCENTAGE OF ALL CROPLAND, 1959

By State-parts of Water Resource Regions

★ = LESS THAN 1%
EASTERN AVERAGE = 1%
WESTERN AVERAGE = 14%
U.S. AVERAGE = 7.5%
HAWAII = 45%
ALASKA = LESS THAN 1%

U. S. DEPARTMENT OF AGRICULTURE

NEG. ERS 3534-65 (2) ECONOMIC RESEARCH SERVICE

Figure 3

accordance with various hypotheses on the extent to which privately and publicly undertaken development in each region might be dissuaded. No judgments are made on the propriety of such constraints actually being invoked.

Historical and Projective Growth Functions

Growth functions have been synthesized for each of the 22 major water resource regions and the two region groupings of the United States as shown in figure 3. The eastern mainland is taken to include the Upper Mississippi, Lower Missouri, Lower Arkansas, Lower Mississippi, and all regions east thereof--13 regions in all. The western mainland includes the remaining 9 regions. Data for Hawaii and Alaska have been considered, but acceptable functions for these two States could not be derived. They are omitted from this summary report, except as noted later.

The total time span of the analysis is from the year 1939 (the beginning of the historical acreage series) to the year 2000. The period 1939-59 encloses the historical series of five observed acreages published (6) or developed (2) as necessary for each region for 1939, 1944, 1949, 1954, and 1959. For ease of computation, the year 1949 as the midpoint of the historical series is taken as the statistical origin of trends and also retained as the mathematical origin of the time variable t in regional long-term growth functions. That is, $t = (year - 1949)/5$, so that $t(1939) = -2$, $t(1944) = 1$, $t(1949) = 0$, $t(1954) = 1$, and $t(1959) = 2$. The latter as the most recent year of published record is the point of departure in projecting growth functions to $t(2000) = 10.2$.

DERIVATION PROCEDURE

Incorporating the concept of eventual acreage limits balanced against trends computed for 1939-59, the basic projective growth function for any region or group of regions is

(1) $A_t = L - \left[(L - A_2) e^{B(t-2)}\right]$, $e = 2.71828$, $t \geqslant 2$.

A_t is the acreage projected for any future time t. It is the difference between the parameter L (the eventual limit specified) and that part of L not reached by time t; namely, less the bracketed portion of (1). The latter depends in turn on the potential acreage remaining in 1959, $(L - A_2)$, when $t = 2$, and on the proportion of $(L - A_2)$ estimated to remain in years beyond 1959 when $t > 2$. Call this proportion $e^{B(t-2)}$ the damping factor, which is unity in 1959 when $t = 2$. It decreases asymptotically toward zero as t increases indefinitely. Thus, the limiting acreage not reached in distant years tends to zero, or is negligibly damped, and A_t approaches L.

Assigning the factor $t-2$ in (1), to give $e^{B(t-2)}$ a value of 1 for 1959 when t was 2, links any historical function ending in 1959 to its corresponding projective function beginning in 1959.

The parameter B in (1) represents the continuous constant percentage decline in remaining potential, imputed from the average percentage decline in remaining potential noted between 1954 and 1959 as the most recent interval of record, when t ranged from $+1$ for 1954 to $+2$ for 1959. This basis for projecting B beyond 1959 is given explicitly by

(2) $(L - A_2) = (L - A_1) e^B$, in which

(3) $B = \log_e \left[(L - A_2) / (L - A_1)\right]$

With B and t thus known, the damping factor as used in (1) is taken from standard tables of $e^x = e^{B(t-2)}$.

Recognizing that the terms A, L, and B in (1) to (3) have unique values for each water resource region i, the aggregation of (1) to totals for the eastern mainland (E), the western mainland (W), and the United States (US) is simply

(4) $A_t (US) = A_t(E) + A_t (W)$
$$= \sum_{i=1}^{13} A_t (i) + \sum_{i=14}^{22} A_t (i).$$

Composite projective growth functions for region groupings can also be fitted directly. Results either way did not differ substantially in this study, but significance tests did consider directly fitted historical functions.

The historical function for 1939-59 for any region from which A_1 and A_2 are computed in calculating $L-A_1$, $L-A_2$, and B in (3) is expressed as

(5) $\quad A_t = a\, b^t\, c^{t^2},\ -2 \leqslant t \leqslant 2,\ t = (\text{year} - 1949)/5.$

This complex exponential allows for variable or invariable percentage rates of change in A_t, depending on the statistical significance of the coefficients. Other functions, including $A_t = a + bt + ct^2$, were also considered in preliminary graphic plotting, but appeared to be less appropriate.

The constants a, b, and c in (5) are evaluated with least-squares techniques, determining the regression of acreage reported in the $N = 5$ censuses of 1939, 1944, 1949, 1954, and 1959 on time, for simplicity using Fisher's method of orthogonal polynomials (1).

The orthogonal equation is

(6) $\quad \log A_t' = \log a' + \log b'\, \xi_1 + \log c'\, \xi_2.$

where for all regions $\xi_1 = t$ (since N is odd), and $\xi_2 = t^2 - 2$. The standard logarithmic form of (5) is

(7) $\quad \log A_t = \log a + \log bt + \log ct^2.$

For this analysis it can be shown (1) that

(8) $\quad \log a = \log a' - 2\log c = 1/5 \sum\limits_{t\,=\,-2}^{2} (\log \underline{A}_t) - 2\log c$

(9) $\quad \log b = \log b' = 1/5 \sum\limits_{t\,=\,-2}^{2} (t\log \underline{A}_t)$

(10) $\quad \log c = \log c' = 1/14 \sum\limits_{t\,=\,-2}^{2} (t^2 - 2)\, \underline{A}_t$

The $\underline{A}_t$ in (8), (9), and (10) denote acreages reported in the Census of Agriculture as contrasted with A_t, the computed acreage for time t.

HISTORICAL GROWTH RATES

Because the historical growth functions are necessary to estimate A_2, A_1, and B in the projective function (1), the historical estimators are discussed first. Table 1 sum-

Table 1.--Estimators of regional irrigation in the United States, 1939-59

Water resource regions	[1] $A_t = ab^t c^{t^2}$		Annual acreage change[3]	
			1939	1959
	[2]a	b		
			Percent	Percent
New England..........	31	1.7513	50.40	-6.35
Delaware and Hudson...	47	1.8108	12.61	12.61
Chesapeake Bay.......	12	2.0291	15.20	15.20
Southeast............	380	1.4477	17.50	2.19
Eastern Great Lakes...	10	1.5971	9.82	9.82
Western Great Lakes...	15	1.9743	22.04	10.26
Ohio Basin[4].........	12	1.6043	9.91	9.91
Cumberland[4].........	1	1.6043	9.91	9.91
Tennessee Basin[4].....	11	1.6043	9.91	9.91
Upper Mississippi.....	17	1.8426	13.80	13.80
Lower Mississippi.....	243	1.5152	8.67	8.67
Lower Missouri........	1	3.8730	31.10	31.10
Lower Arkansas........	290	1.4990	8.43	8.43
Eastern mainland....	1,070	1.4040	7.02	7.02
Upper Missouri........	4,605	1.1397	2.65	2.65
Upper Arkansas........	1,010	1.4105	3.39	9.42
Western Gulf..........	2,976	1.4859	14.96	3.97
Upper Rio Grande......	1,042	1.1169	2.24	2.24
Colorado Basin........	2,848	1.0374	0.74	0.74
Great Basin..........	1,740	1.0477	0.94	0.94
Pacific Northwest.....	3,894	1.1069	2.05	2.05
Central Pacific.......	5,239	1.1428	4.87	1.43
South Pacific........	641	1.1360	2.69	2.69
Western mainland....	23,995	1.1254	2.39	2.39
United States........	25,065	1.1436	2.72	2.72

[1] A_t = computed thousands of acres irrigated at time $t \leq 2$; $t = (\text{year} - 1949)/5$. The term 'c' was significant (≥ 80 percent level in F statistics) for only 6 regions, as follows: New England (0.74373); Southeast (0.91640); Western lakes (0.93883); Upper Arkansas (1.03610); Western Gulf (0.93513); and Central Pacific (0.97941).
[2] Thousands of acres irrigated in 1949, when $t = 0$.
[3] Significant variable rates of increase between 1939 and 1959 underscored; significant constant rates not underscored.
[4] Ohio, Cumberland, and Tennessee regions pooled in computing 'b' and 'c'.

marizes the statistical analysis of irrigated acreage in each of the 22 mainland water resource regions and presents trend estimators converted to their natural form corresponding to (5).

The annual rates of increase estimated in table 1 lend quantification to regional shifts in irrigation (and associated water use) observed since World War II. Along with an average annual national increase of 2.72 percent, there was a marked relative shift to the eastern mainland associated with the annual increase there of 7.02 percent. However, the current acreage in the East is still only about 7 percent of the U.S. total. And in the East there was a pronounced shift to the Lower

Missouri, Chesapeake, Upper Mississippi, and Delaware-Hudson regions and, with the exception of New England, some shifts in all eastern regions at the expense of the Southeast. However, about 25 percent of all eastern irrigation in 1959 was still in the Southeast States, with another 25 percent in the Lower Mississippi Valley, and 30 percent in Lower Arkansas. Note the decreasing rate of increase in the Western Lakes region.

For the western mainland, with 93 percent of the total national acreage in 1959, a large part of the 2.39 percent annual increase between 1939 and 1959 was due to new irrigation development in the Upper Arkansas, Western Gulf, and Upper Missouri regions. Together these accounted for about 42 percent of the acreage irrigated in the West in 1959. The annual rate of increase itself increased in the Upper Arkansas--from 3.39 percent per year in 1939 to 9.42 percent in 1959. The yearly increase in the Western Gulf, however, fell from nearly 15 percent annually in 1939 to around 4 percent in 1959. This was due in part to depletion of ground water reserves in the High Plains of Western Texas. The Central Valley of California, currently accounting for 20 percent of all western irrigation and thus for between 18 and 19 percent of all the irrigated land in the United States, experienced a similar drop in its increase rate, from 4.87 percent per year in 1939 down to 1.43 percent in 1959. Urbanization, nearly full use of readily available water supplies, and other factors explain the relative decline in this irrigated region.

Economic Limits to Irrigation

In this study, the economic limit to irrigated acreage in each water resource region was construed to be the maximum acreage of soils feasibly irrigated (i.e., costs ≥ benefits at the extensive margin), given prevailing notions of natural moisture and yearly (or seasonal) moisture deficiencies, future irrigation returns in relation to costs, and foreseen limits on water supplies. With respect to the definition accepted, the studies of the Department of Agriculture for the Senate Select Committee on National Water Resources (6), the Depart-

ment's own National Inventory of Soil and Water Conservation Needs (7), and a study by the Bureau of Reclamation (3) are relevant. Moreover, these works either directly or indirectly (and fairly independently) consider remaining potentials as divided into two major components: (a) The additional acreage irrigable from water supplies feasibly developed by individual farm operators, local irrigation districts, or State agencies; and (b) the additional acreage irrigable from water supplies feasibly developed in connection with large-scale multipurpose water projects, with Federal financing a matter of considerable importance.

Estimates of remaining irrigation potentials given in these studies have been collated and summarized by regions in table 2. In general, the remaining Federal potentials in the East are assumed to be limited by the acreages possibly irrigated with Federal assistance authorized by the multipurpose Watershed Protection and Flood Prevention Act (P.L. 83-566). Although this Act applies to all States and Puerto Rico, remaining Federal potentials in the West are approximated both from the

Table 2.--Remaining irrigation potentials in 1959 in the United States with Federal and non-Federal distribution

Water resource regions	Total	Federal	Non-Federal
	1,000 acres	Percent	Percent
New England.........	106	30	70
Delaware and Hudson.	288	36	64
Chesapeake Bay......	622	21	79
Southeast...........	4,515	45	55
Eastern Great Lakes.	284	42	58
Western Great Lakes.	456	7	93
Ohio Basin..........	922	32	68
Cumberland..........	14	76	24
Tennessee Basin.....	206	34	66
Upper Mississippi...	1,125	15	85
Lower Mississippi...	3,365	17	83
Lower Missouri......	1,212	9	91
Lower Arkansas......	2,309	26	74
Eastern mainland..	15,504	28	72
Upper Missouri......	4,819	84	16
Upper Arkansas.....	2,436	36	64
Western Gulf........	3,174	96	4
Upper Rio Grande....	738	100	0
Colorado Basin......	925	96	4
Great Basin.........	757	78	22
Pacific Northwest...	4,515	85	15
Central Pacific.....	6,721	32	68
South Pacific.......	847	13	87
Western mainland..	24,932	65	35
United States.......	40,436	51	49

USDA Conservation Needs Inventory and from Bureau of Reclamation investigations.

For the eastern regions as a group, table 2 indicates that roughly 75 percent of the remaining acreage potentials can be developed independently by individual farm operators. Federal assistance through multipurpose small watershed programs under P.L. 566 is seen to have its greatest probable importance for supplemental irrigation in the Southeast, Lower Mississippi, and Lower Arkansas regions, considering both the percentages and acreages involved.

For the western regions, where Bureau of Reclamation projects now include about one-fourth of the total area irrigated, table 2 shows that roughly two-thirds of the remaining acreage potential is associated with Federal projects that may be completed, with new Federal reclamation of greatest relative importance to the Colorado, Western Gulf, Pacific Northwest, and Upper Missouri regions. Future State activity is of notable importance in California. The Upper Arkansas region stands out as perhaps most important from the standpoint of additional private development in the West.

For the United States as a whole, table 2 indicates that the expansion of irrigated acreage seems about equally dependent on Federal and non-Federal activity. Total remaining potentials by region in table 2 are added to acreages computed for 1959 in column 1 of table 3 to indicate the maximum economic limits to irrigation in the various regions (L_{100} in col. 4 of table 3). The derived limits as constrained are given in the columns headed by L_{25} and L_{50} in table 3.

Alternative Policies and Long-Term Growth Functions

Alternative policies and their possible consequences are reviewed here in terms of the basic growth function (1). They are considered in decreasing order of stringency with respect to future irrigation growth, and thus in increasing order of acreages irrigated at specified dates. Figure 4 illustrates aggregate U.S. historical and long-term functions, with the latter conditioned by the three policies considered. Some detail for the East, the West, and the

Table 3.--Irrigation in 1959 and regional limits on irrigation in the United States based on selected proportions of remaining Federal and non-Federal potentials over 1959 being developed

Water resource regions	1959[1]	Regional limits[2]		
	A_2	L_{25}	L_{50}	L_{100}
	1,000 acres	*1,000 acres*	*1,000 acres*	*1,000 acres*
New England...........	29	74	82	135
Delaware and Hudson...	147	265	291	435
Chesapeake Bay........	49	327	360	671
Southeast.............	561	2,309	2,818	5,076
Eastern Great Lakes...	26	139	168	310
Western Great Lakes...	45	265	273	501
Ohio Basin...........	30	416	491	952
Cumberland...........	3	44	50	97
Tennessee Basin.......	28	114	131	234
Upper Mississippi.....	57	576	620	1,182
Lower Mississippi.....	559	2,102	2,242	3,924
Lower Missouri........	13	592	619	1,225
Lower Arkansas........	651	1,657	1,806	2,960
Eastern mainland....	2,198	8,880	9,951	17,702
Upper Missouri........	5,981	7,379	8,390	10,800
Upper Arkansas........	2,315	3,314	3,533	4,751
Western Gulf..........	5,024	5,852	6,611	8,198
Upper Rio Grande......	1,300	1,484	1,671	2,038
Colorado Basin........	3,065	3,305	3,528	3,990
Great Basin...........	1,910	2,141	2,289	2,667
Pacific Northwest.....	4,770	6,063	7,028	9,285
Central Pacific.......	6,296	9,110	9,657	13,017
South Pacific.........	827	1,223	1,251	1,674
Western mainland....	31,488	39,871	43,958	56,420
United States.........	33,686	48,751	53,909	74,122

[1] Computed as shown in and transferred from table 1.
[2] L_{25} assumes eventual development of 25 percent of remaining Federal potentials but 50 percent development of remaining non-Federal (private and State) potentials; L_{50} assumes both Federal and non-Federal development at 50 percent of their remaining potentials; and L_{100} assumes 100 percent for both.

United States as a whole is given in table 4, for 1959, 1964, 1980, and 2000.

L_{25}--minimal Federal and modest non-Federal development:

This limit, assumed to be operational in 1959-2000, identifies successful efforts to hold the eventual area irrigated in all regions to a level such that only 25 percent of the remaining Federal potentials shown in table 2 would be developed, and such that 50 percent of the remaining non-Federal potentials would be irrigated.

56

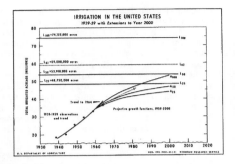

IRRIGATION IN THE UNITED STATES
1939-59 with Extensions to Year 2000

Figure 4

Table 4.--Selected estimates of irrigated acreage in the United States, 1959 to 2000, based on reported Census data, 1939-59 trends, and alternative long-term limits

Year and basis	Eastern mainland	Western mainland	United States
	Million acres	*Million acres*	*Million acres*
1959:			
Reported............	1.87	31.15	[1] 33.02
1939-59 trend.......	2.20	31.50	[2] 33.70
1964:			
1939-59 trend......	3.09	35.44	[3] 38.53
A_{25} (on L_{25})........	2.74	33.86	[4] 36.60
A_{50} (on L_{50}).......	2.75	34.22	36.97
A_{100} (on L_{100}).....	2.78	34.65	37.43
1980:			
A_{25} (on L_{25})........	4.06	37.34	41.40
A_{50} (on L_{50}).......	4.15	39.10	43.25
A_{100} (on L_{100}).....	4.41	41.80	46.21
2000:			
A_{25} (on L_{25})........	5.15	38.75	43.90
A_{50} (on L_{50}).......	5.30	41.65	46.95
A_{100} (on L_{100}).....	6.05	47.00	53.05

[1] Add 141,000 acres for Hawaii and 360 acres for Alaska.
[2] Data insufficient for Alaska and trend not significant for Hawaii. U.S. total is about 33.88 with reported data for these States added.
[3] U.S. total is about 38.71 if 1959 reported acreages for Hawaii and Alaska are added.
[4] Hawaii and Alaska excluded from consideration in this and subsequent U.S. totals.

For each region the long-run growth function (1) now has the form:

$$(11) \quad A_t = L_{25} - (L_{25} - A_2) e^{B(t-2)}, \quad t \geq 2, \text{(year} \geq 1959).$$

From tables 1 and 3 the empirical function (A_t in millions of acres) for the mainland 48 States is approximately

$$(12) \quad A_t = 48.751 - 15.065 e^{-0.175(t-2)}.$$

By evaluating (12) for any year beyond 1959, the long-run consequences of a hypothesis of minimal Federal and modest non-Federal development in the United States can be estimated. The time path of irrigated acreage between 1959 and 2000 conditioned by this hypothesis is plotted as the curve A_{25} in figure 4. Subscripts in this chart and also in table 4 now refer to controlling limits over time, rather than to time t as such.

As expected, this hypothesis (combined with a recognition of past growth rates) indicates an accelerated relative shift of irrigation to the Eastern States, with the East accounting for about 12 percent of the total U.S. acreage projected to the year 2000. At that time about 58 percent of the limit L_{25} would be reached in the eastern mainland, 97 percent of the corresponding western limit would be reached, and, nationally, 90 percent of the L_{25} limit would be reached. But in relation to maximum economic potentials the percentages for the year 2000 would be considerably lower; that

is, 29 percent for the East, 69 percent for the West, and 59 percent nationally.

L_{50}--modest Federal and non-Federal development:

This limit identifies efforts to hold the eventual area irrigated in all regions to a level such that 50 percent of both the remaining Federal and non-Federal potentials given in table 2 would be developed. As constrained by this limit the long-run growth function (1) for any region has the form

$$(13) \quad A_t = L_{50} - (L_{50} - A_2) e^{B(t-2)}, \quad t \geq 2, \text{year} \geq 1959,$$

and from tables 1 and 3 for the United States we have, in millions of acres,

$$(14) \quad A_t = 53.909 - 20.223 e^{-0.145(t-2)}.$$

By evaluating (14) for any year, beginning with 1959, the time path of irrigated acreage in the United States is approximately as shown by the curve A_{50} in figure 4. Projections on this hypothesis imply a continued relative shift of irrigated acreage to the Eastern States (11 percent of the U.S. total in the year 2000 compared with 7 percent in 1959). The shift is associated more with continuation of the rapid eastern rate of increase observed between 1939 and 1959 than with relatively greater encouragement of non-Federal irrigation that would favor the East, as was hypothesized in L_{25} above. This hypothesis shows also that if remaining Federal and non-Federal development is only modestly and proportionately constrained in all regions, western irrigation would reach about 75 percent of its maximum economic potential by the year 2000, and the United States would reach 63 percent of its maximum potential.

L_{100}--unconstrained Federal and non-Federal development:

This limit implies that eventual irrigation would approximate the maximum economic limits identified as L_{100} in table 3. On this hypothesis, eventual irrigation in the East could be eight times the 1959 acreage, in the West it could be 80 percent more than the current acreage, and for the United States it could be about 2-1/5 times the current acreage.

As influenced only by past trends and the economic limits defined, the long-run growth function (1) for any region has the form

(15) $A_t = L_{100} - (L_{100} - A^2) e^{B(t-2)}$, $t \geqslant 2$, year $\geqslant 1959$.

and from tables 1 and 3 we have in millions of acres for the United States

(16) $A_{t_|} = 74.122 - 40.436 e^{-0.085(t-2)}$.

Evaluations of (16) generate the time path of irrigated acreage shown as the A_{100} curve in figure 4.

Differential relative rates of growth during 1939-59, and the relative as well as the absolute magnitudes of remaining Federal and non-Federal irrigation potentials in each region, all influence this projection in an undetermined way. But the net result for the year 2000 is still a decided relative shift to the Eastern States, substantial increases in acreage in both the East and the West (175 and 49 percent over 1959, respectively), and an overall

national increase to about 53 million acres compared with the 33 million acres computed for 1959 (table 4). Within this procedure, the 6 million acres irrigated in the East at that time would be 34 percent of the East's maximum economic potential, compared with 12 percent in 1959. The 47 million acres in the year 2000 projected for the West would be 83 percent of the maximum, compared with 56 percent in 1959. And the national total of 53 million acres in the year 2000 would be about 72 percent of the national economic limit.

Policies Consistent with Dated Requirements

Here we return briefly to irrigation projections made in various studies cited at the outset. Within stated assumptions concerning future population, the urbanization of farmland, related requirements for farm and nonfarm products or services, and other relevant factors, characteristically these studies have computed corresponding requirements for increasing, decreasing, or perhaps leaving unchanged the extent of crop or pasture irrigation in different regions. The relative and absolute productivity of land, water, or other resources at projected levels of technology and management practices have been considered also, but a point commonly stressed is that the projected patterns of resource use are not economic norms. However, they are seen to identify a number of necessary conditions for optimal resource use, and they have contributed a great deal of information needed by legislators and other policymakers. This raises a question as to whether the research described here can be useful in identifying constraints on eventual irrigation development in different regions or in the country generally that would result in specified acreages being irrigated by specified dates. The foregoing system of regional relations in historical rates of irrigation and remaining Federal and non-Federal development potentials might be adapted to such problems, somewhat as follows:

Assume that 45 million acres of irrigated land have been recommended as the optimal acreage for the United States in 1980. This is roughly midway between the acreages previously calculated for 1980 from the long-run growth function conditioned by modest Federal and non-Federal development (14), and the function (16) unconstrained by any limitations on eventual economic development. The basic growth function (1) is utilized in this case to solve for L, with $t-2 = 4.2$ for 1980 given, and with $A_2 = 33.686$ millions of acres for 1959 also known. Our "constant" of 45 million acres is the dashed vertical line in figure 5.

Graphic interpolation is appropriate here, since B varies in (2) not only with L as the limit being sought, but also with A_1 and A_2 as the acreages computed for both 1954 and 1959; respectively, 29.274 and 33.686 million acres. The earlier results of exploring hypothetical policy limits are useful for getting a solution here too, since there is a proportional relation between acreages projected for given dates and the ratio $[(L - A_2)/(L - A_1)]$. This rela-

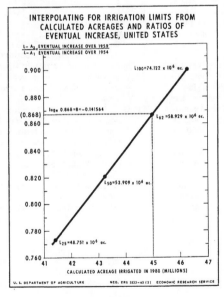

INTERPOLATING FOR IRRIGATION LIMITS FROM CALCULATED ACREAGES AND RATIOS OF EVENTUAL INCREASE, UNITED STATES

Figure 5

tion is illustrated in figure 5 for the year 19 on the basis of three coordinate "observation identified with the three previously specifi limits L_{25}, L_{50}, and L_{100}.

With the additional information in figure the function (1) can be written and solved f L, as follows:

$$(17) \quad 45.000 = L - (L - 33.686) e^{-0.141564(4.2)}, \text{ or}$$

$$45.000 = L - (L - 33.686)(0.5518), \text{ and}$$

$$L = 26.412/0.448200 = 59 \text{ million acres} \\ \text{(approx.).}$$

Thus, the procedure for deriving lon term growth functions that recognize b the inertial effects of historical trends a the damping effects of controlling limits irrigation suggests that a hypothetical poli aimed at eventual irrigation of about million acres in the United States wo result in about 45 million acres being i rigated in the year 1980 (see fig. 4, for 1980). The derived limit of 59 milli acres implies that about 62 percent of t total remaining Federal and non-Federal p tential of 40.4 million acres given in table would be developed eventually; that is, L_{62} the dashed horizontal in figure 4 is 59 milli acres.

Reversing the procedure again yields continuous growth function or time path irrigation between the present and 1980, si ply by substituting for L the derived li of 59 million acres in equation (1) as app cable to the United States, and then solving A_t as desired. Results are the dashed cu A' in figure 4.

Other Applications and Concluding Comments

If one could assess the likelihood over ti of various "policy" limits being set on futu irrigated acreage, such a probability distrib tion of irrigation policy could be used to obt an approximate probability function for da estimates of irrigated acreage also. In t sense, the growth functions A_{25}, A_{50}, and A_{100} in figure 4 are examples of discrete events to be considered in such derivations.

Pending these derivations one can only say that, if L_{25} and L_{100} are reasonable limits to the actual policy limits set, A_{25} and A_{100} are reasonable limits of actual time paths of acreage, with specific probabilities of occurrence unknown. The seriousness of this and other limitations decreases with a decreasing propensity to project,[3] so there is some justification for using the procedures to obtain short-term intercensus estimates of irrigated acreage that recognize historical trends and possible long-term limits. Thus, advance estimates of the U.S. acreage to be reported from the 1964 Census of Agriculture could be given as the range 36.6–38.5 million acres, with the lower figure being the 1964 value of the A_{25} function in figure 4 and the upper one being an extrapolation of the 1939-59 trend (see table 4). Of course, synoptic observations of regional precipitation, snowpack accumulations, reservoir storage, cost-price relations, and other factors for 1964 would suggest deviations from or lend more validity to such interval estimates.

Another limitation of the analysis is that the hypothetical policy limits have been applied across the board to all regions. Interregional variations in national policy can be expected even if not intended. Their possible effects on regional irrigation development would be interesting to explore also.

A final limitation noted here is that the methods outlined have only partly allowed for pending State and Federal projects for transregion water diversions and other technological developments, so the given economic limits to irrigation are perhaps too static. Results should be interpreted accordingly, although the methods are quite accommodative to the availability of more and better information.

---

[3] To illustrate: For the year 2000 the U.S. projected acreage on A_{25} in figure 4 is about 6 percent under the projection on A_{50} while the projection on A_{100} is 13 percent over the A_{50} projection. Deviations from A_{50} similarly computed for 1980 drop to the range -4 and +7 percent, and for 1964 drop to between -2 and +3 percent (see table 4).

Literature Cited

(1) Anderson, R. L., and E. E. Houseman. Tables of orthogonal polynomial values extended to n-104. Iowa Agr. Expt. Sta., Res. Bul. 297, Ames, 1942.

(2) Bureau of the Census. U.S. Census of Agriculture: 1959. Vol. II, General report; vol. III, Irrigation of agricultural lands. U.S. Dept. Commerce, 1962.

(3) Bureau of Reclamation. Water resources activities in the United States: Future needs for reclamation in the Western States. 86th Cong., 2d Sess., Senate Select Committee on National Water Resources, Committee Print No. 14, 1960.

(4) Headley, J. C., and V. W. Ruttan. Regional differences in the impact of irrigation on farm output. In: Economics and Public Policy in Water Resource Development, S. C. Smith and E. N. Castle (eds.), pp. 127-149, Iowa State Univ. Press, Ames, 1964.

(5) Landsberg, Hans H., Leonard L. Fischman, and Joseph L. Fisher. Resources in America's future; patterns of requirements and availabilities, 1960-2000. Published for Resources for the Future, Inc., by Johns Hopkins Press, Baltimore, 1963.

(6) U.S. Department of Agriculture. Water resources activities in the United States: Land and water potentials and future requirements for water. 86th Cong., 1st Sess., Senate Select Committee on National Water Resources, Comm. Print No. 12, 1959.

(7) U.S. Department of Agriculture. Soil and water conservation needs--a national inventory. Misc. Pub. 971, 94 pp., 1965.

(8) U.S. Department of Agriculture. Land and water resources--a policy guide. Land and Water Policy Committee, 1962.

(9) U.S. Senate. Report of the Select Committee on National Water Resources. 87th Cong., 1st Sess., Senate Rpt. 29, 63 pp., 1961.

(10) Wooten, Hugh H., Karl Gertel, and William C. Pendleton. Major uses of land and water in the United States; summary for 1959. U.S. Dept. Agr., Agr. Econ. Rpt. 13, 54 pp., July 1962.

Book Reviews

War Against Want

By George S. McGovern. Walker and Company, New York. 148 pages. 1964. $5.

AS PRESIDENT Lyndon B. Johnson points out in the Foreword, Senator McGovern writes about hunger and ways of relieving it from a rich background of experience. As an educator, Congressman and now Senator from an agricultural State, and former Food for Peace Director, Senator McGovern has had an impressive opportunity to grapple, firsthand, with the world paradox of surplus and want.

The need to provide more food for hungry people is presented in a way that should stir the conscience of affluent and overfed American readers who are accustomed to scolding their children about not eating their dinners, while both they and their children are unaware that most children of the world go to bed hungry. In the author's words, "We live in a crisis of abundance in a world of want."

The world need for more food is well documented and the activities of the present-day Food for Peace Program are effectively and sympathetically presented. Senator McGovern is impressed with the many successes that have been achieved by the present food aid programs, but he realizes that current efforts are not sufficient to fill the nutritional gap. At the end of the book, he presents a 10-point program for using our abundance more effectively to help fill the current food gap, and more importantly, to assist food-short countries in expanding their domestic food output. His 10-point program is summarized as follows:

1. Greatly enlarge the U.S. Food for Peace Program.

2. Adopt an agricultural policy which will foster increased--not decreased--production.

3. Place greater emphasis on nutritional standards in the Food for Peace Program.

4. Remove all political restrictions on Food for Peace shipments to foreign countries--even Communist countries.

5. Enlarge the School Lunch Program to cover every needy child in the world.

6. At least triple the number of "food-for-wages" projects in the developing world.

7. Use a larger percentage of foreign currencies generated by Food for Peace sales, plus foreign aid funds, to improve good distribution facilities.

8. Make greater use of Peace Corps volunteers in the Food for Peace effort.

9. Place greater emphasis on agricultural development in the foreign aid program.

10. Increase U.S. participation in such international efforts as "The Freedom From Hunger Campaign."

Senator McGovern realizes that the only permanent protection against hunger is development of self-sustaining economies in the food-short countries--economies which can either produce food enough for their people or earn foreign exchange to pay for commercial imports of food. This problem is discussed under Point 9 of his 10-point program.

This reviewer would have appreciated more emphasis on how to use food aid as an effective tool for economic development. This requires a partnership of donor and recipient countries, and both parties must be willing and able to carry out their parts of the bargain. A stable government, good leadership, and a determination to carry out the necessary program are essential to progress in food-short countries. Attempts at rapid expansion of food aid are likely to encounter many frustrations in countries lacking these requisites for progress. But Senator McGovern would emphasize the serious consequences of neglecting any feasible opportunities for the use of food aid in economic development.

"War Against Want" is an informative and readable account of our present Food for Peace Program. It is also a challenge to increase our efforts, despite anticipated difficulties.

Sherman E. Johnson

Hungry Nations

By William and Paul Paddock. Little, Brown and Company, Boston. 344 pages. 1964. $6.50

THE PADDOCK BROTHERS have four decades of work in the "hungry nations." They call the underdeveloped countries "hungry nations" because they are hungry for food, they are hungry for stability, they are hungry for international prestige, for education, for health, housing, and culture. They are hungry for the twentieth century. The authors have arrived at a definite idea on why these nations are hungry; they do not have sufficient resources in proportion to the size of the population to create a surplus. If nations are to progress, their resources must produce more than their people can use. It is these surpluses that will determine their prosperity. Yet future prosperity in the hungry nations will probably be rather moderate because the resources, unfortunately, are moderate--whether agricultural lands, minerals, natural harbors, or whatever.

The Paddocks look at traditional development programs, whether initiated by local governments or foreign aid funds, and analyze the fallacies embedded in these programs that bring to naught the efforts expended. They make the following criticisms:

(1) Slum clearance merely makes the city more attractive to poverty-stricken farm area inhabitants. No matter how much is spent for this program, slums will always develop in the cities until the rural areas are made more attractive to live in.

(2) A public health program actually damages the economy of a backward nation and definitely delays, if it does not eliminate, hope for a rise in living standards until population control is effectively organized. A life without ills is a luxury countries cannot afford until they cease to be hungry.

(3) Surplus food shipments are no favor to a country, until it gets its population back to a livable ratio with its farm production. This merely postpones elimination of surplus population. The world rushes to help hungry children but is callous toward the conditions in which those same children must live after they become adults and are still hungry.

(4) Education in present-day European and American style is a luxury which a hungry nation cannot afford. It must be practical, designed to help the people produce more. Graduate study should be done in countries which can afford adequate schools.

(5) Industrialization does not reduce hunger or poverty, except for a favored few. Each successfully industrialized nation had both mineral resources and fertile land which enabled farmers to produce a surplus to feed the new industrial workers.

(6) Rich countries can afford social reforms, but for the poor ones reforms can be the death stroke.

(7) Land reform is carried out as social reform, instead of being designed to provide maximum land utilization.

(8) Road building should follow development, not precede it.

(9) The difference between foreign aid for political purposes and long-range resource development of backward countries has not been recognized. We do not know how to develop these countries and eliminate world hunger.

The authors suggest some guidelines, perhaps idealistic, for reducing the despair and privations of a hungry nation. All the nation's efforts, all its capital reserves and foreign exchange, all its internal and international policies must be devoted single-mindedly to this one project: make the nation's resources produce surpluses. Each hungry nation must itself develop the research that will develop its resources, that will "alter the hand of God." It cannot directly transfer to its own problems the techniques and solutions developed in other areas of the world.

At home, they suggest dividing the foreign aid program into two parts. The political foreign aid would include all those programs designed to carry out our foreign policy. To aid in the development of resources of the hungry nations, they propose a Bureau of Foreign Resource Development, somewhat similar to the National Institute for Educational and Technical Cooperation proposed in the Gardner Report (AID and the universities).

The book is very readable and well documented without a lot of statistics. It is certain to have an impact on thinking people concerned with foreign economic development. Hopefully, it will be educational to those readers the authors hope to attract, the leaders or future leaders of the hungry nations.

Quentin M. West

Economic Development

By John Kenneth Galbraith. Harvard University Press, Cambridge. 109 pages. 1964. $2.95.

ECONOMIC DEVELOPMENT a la Professor Galbraith is interesting, candid, and sharply analytical. The student of economic development may find little that is new in these lectures. But he will enjoy the penetrating analysis of development problems, without benefit of sophisticated econometric models, as well as the wit and skill of a master of the English language.

Galbraith tells of some of his frustrations as an ambassador in matters relating to public expression when he explains the origin of the book and his decision to prepare a series of lectures on economic development. The lectures were delivered at all major universities of India and widely published in daily papers.

Usually the underdeveloped country cannot afford a wholly unguided or undifferentiated growth. And such symbols of modernization as airlines, impressive buildings, and a steel industry often are not consistent with the needs of the country. His solution is a goal which "anchors economic development to consumption requirements, present and prospective, of the typical citizen" or the modal consumer. His "Popular Consumption Criterion" concentrates the attention of the planner on the needs of the most numerous or typical citizen.

The needs of the average citizen are not the only points upon which the planner should concentrate more attention. In our approach to causes of stagnation and national poverty we have been very casual, compared with the vigor and thoroughness with which we attack the problems of space, for example. Despite our sophisticated work on economic growth, we do not have an analytical framework which explains stagnation. Professor Galbraith considers the many assumptions on the causes of poverty. After pointing out inconsistencies and limited applicability of the causes now used as a basis for many of our remedies, he is pessimistic. Men may reach the moon in the next few years, and "hopefully the righteous among them will return," but the most acute problem of this planet will remain unsolved. Professor Galbraith concludes that the common denominator of progress is a liberated and educated people. We are coming to realize, he feels, "that there is a certain sterility in economic monuments that stand alone in a sea of illiteracy."

Even with our advanced growth models, the author feels we have been looking only at the parts and too infrequently at whether these parts fit into a viable whole. We observe the need for know-how, capital, and a sound plan, but our diagnosis often fails to consider such strategic limiting factors as effective government, education, and social justice.

Professor Galbraith looks on economic aid as a cooperative endeavor in which each country has something to offer. But exchanges of technology are not without danger, particularly to the borrower. It is much easier to transfer seed and fertilizer or even a complicated machine than to transfer organization and services. In developing this latter point, the author observes that it was the unquestioned good fortune of the United States a hundred years ago that "community education experts, grain marketing analysts, home economists, vocational counselors, communication specialists, or public safety advisers had not been invented."

The author focuses sharply and effectively on the planning debate. He demonstrates that all modern nations have plans, but they differ in the degree to which plans are avowed, in the formality with which goals are spelled out, and particularly in the techniques used to achieve goals. Professor Galbraith feels there is no

63

alternative to state initiative when "a great leap forward" is necessary. Space exploration is such an example in the U.S. economy. But the building of a steel mill or hydroelectric plant may be an equally great leap in the underdeveloped economy. Planning takes on a special significance for the underdeveloped economy concerned with such basics as hunger, disease, and urgent needs for housing, education, improved transportation, and communication.

An extended discussion of the requirements of the "good plan" includes an excellent treatment of the need for a sense of strategy--the need for scheduling investment and for matching and phasing various segments of the plan.

The industrial corporation plays a strategic part in economic development, according to the author. Where any productive task must be performed, "the firm is ubiquitous and inescapable." To be effective, the industrial firms must be free to make everyday decisions, but must be held strictly accountable for results.

Many development economists and those in foreign aid administration will not agree with all the analyses, ideas, and, in some cases, biases of Professor Galbraith. But they will find this brief book of essays conveys a wealth of experience, wisdom, and common sense, deftly--and often humorously--expressed.

Rex F. Daly

Economic Growth in the West -- Comparative Experience in Europe and North America

By Angus Maddison. Twentieth Century Fund, New York. 1964. 246 pages. $4.50.

A NGUS MADDISON has drawn upon his experiences with the Organization for European Economic Cooperation and the Organization for Economic Cooperation and Development in presenting this intensive and enlightening study. In it, he contrasts the growth experiences of the Western European countries with those of the United States and the United Kingdom. His analysis seeks to explain why the U.S. and U.K. growth rates, measured in per capita output, have lagged behind the accelerated rates experienced in the Western European countries during the postwar years.

His framework is the Harrod-Domar model, a ratio of investment to output divided by the marginal capital-output ratio. Although texts on economic development point out the shortcomings of this model, it is useful for the author's purpose in explaining output levels in terms of investment relationships, and in an analysis concerned with both the demand and supply side of comparative accelerated growth.

Maddison's hypothesis is that for most Western European countries, government policy which directly stimulated and managed effective demand for commodities led to increased productive investment. In the United States, expansion was slow in the 1950's because of reliance on built-in stabilization and on demand mainly for services, along with lack of central policy. The United States experienced downturns in 1949, 1954, 1958, and 1960-61, whereas the absence of recessions in Western Europe enabled a fuller utilization of supply potential. As European expansion took place, profit incentives encouraged a break with archaic habits which inhibited investment. Government policy directed expansion by adjusting tax systems to meet modern fiscal policy, and by increasing public investment and consumption to absorb an increasing labor supply. This uncertainty-reducing government policy stimulated entrepreneurial confidence and activity, thus raising the levels of equilibrium.

The text is heavily documented with statistical evidence from 1870 to the present that contrasts the record of growth among the nine Western European countries. In addition, it illuminates problems of the internal and external mechanisms of integration within the European Free Trade Association and the European Economic Community.

A statistical appendix on employment, investment, output, and population offers the reader a handy reference for research in the economic development of "developed" economies.

The author does not sacrifice thoroughness despite only 193 pages of text. His style is pleasant and readable. His intent in describing recent, contrasting economic growth experiences is valuable not only as a record of historic fact for students of economic development but to anyone involved in "a practical interest in forecasting what the future development of the western industrial economies would be."

Marshall H. Cohen

Agricultural Sciences for the Developing Nations

Edited by A. H. Moseman. American Association for the Advancement of Sciences, Washington, D.C., 232 pages. 1964. $6.75.

BASED ON a symposium held under the auspices of the AAAS in December 1963, this book contains the views of some of the Nation's leading authorities in international agricultural development. The total, however, is not a blueprint for policies or programs that will assure rapid growth of agriculture in the developing countries. Rather, it is a collection of individual experiences from which the contributors have garnered insights into special aspects of the problems involved in modernizing agricultural systems.

The papers are grouped under four headings: Characteristics of Agricultural Systems in Emerging Nations, Research to Devise and Adapt Innovations, Education and Development of Human Resources, and Establishing Indigenous Institutions to Serve Advancing Agriculture. While the headings do not precisely fit the papers listed under them, they do indicate the book's coverage.

If there is a common core to the 12 papers it is the thesis that agricultural development is a part of overall national development and that agriculture cannot be modernized without recasting its societal foundations. The writers are well aware, in the words of F. F. Hill, "that economic development is in large part a matter of human and institutional development—of developing people, and developing institutions through which they can work effectively." The lead paper by Erven Long, "Institutional Factors Limiting Progress in Less Developed Countries," cogently conveys this.

Among some of the other contributions are "Animal Agriculture in the Emerging Nations" by Ralph Phillips, and "Interactions and Agricultural Research in Emerging Nations" by Charles Kellogg.

The concluding paper, by Theodore Schultz, is a capsule version of his recent book. It is concerned with the need for new institutions to achieve economic growth by transforming traditional agriculture. He concludes that the need is for strong agricultural research institutions which will find new high-yield inputs for the kind of farming characterizing the developing countries, and for systems whereby these inputs can be made available to and used by the farmers.

It seems to this reviewer that the emphasis on institutions is appropriate. But none of the papers deal directly with government institutions and administration as they affect agricultural growth. Yet people in the field report that local governments are often the critical factor in the success or failure of any agricultural institution. The importance of public policies in support of agricultural development in the United States, and the central role played by the USDA in the system of State research, education, and extension, suggests the need for candid examination of public policies and governmental administration affecting agriculture in the developing countries.

The variety of topics covered and the stature of the contributors make this a very valuable addition to any collection of books on international development. Dr. Moseman is to be commended for making it possible.

Martin Kriesberg

Regional Planning and Development: A Reader

Edited by John Friedmann and William Alonso. The M.I.T. Press, Cambridge. 722 pages. 1964. $9.75.

THIS BOOK is intended for students and practitioners of regional economic development and related fields. It is an attempt to emphasize a national approach to regional

65

development and to integrate some of the more important contributions to our understanding of space, development, and planning. The volume includes 34 reprinted articles (which in general were selected from American publications of the last decade), an original survey paper by Alonso on location theory, and about 28 pages of editorial comment on the articles and related literature.

The contents are divided into five parts: (1) space and planning; (2) location and spatial organization; (3) theory of regional development; (4) national policy for regional development; and (5) a guide to the literature.

In part 1, papers by Francois Perroux, Lloyd Rodwin, and co-editor Friedmann introduce the more significant concepts and problems of physical and socioeconomic space, development, and planning.

The seven essays in part 2 are concerned with the theory of economic location (the cited Alonso paper and August Lösch's "The Nature of Economic Regions" from the Southern Economic Journal) and with the spatial organization of regions (two articles by geographer Brian Berry and essays by Edward Ullman, Richard Morrill, and John H. Thompson and collaborators).

Four approaches to the explanation of the spatial differentiation of economic growth are represented by the selections of part 3. Included are: the role of natural resources, industries, and external trade (Harvey Perloff and Lowdon Wingo, Douglas North, Charles Tiebout, Robert Baldwin, and Richard Pfister); the influence of population migration (Bernard Okun and Richard Richardson); the function of cities in development (Eric Lampard, John Friedmann, Richard Morse, and Shanti Tangri); and the effects of rural periphery and urban center interaction (two essays by W i l l i a m N i c h o l l s, and papers by Dale Hathaway and the United Nations Department of Economic and Social Affairs).

In part 4 the 11 selections consider the spatial versus functional organization of regional planning (John Friedmann, Paul Ylvisaker, Vincent Ostrom and collaborators, and Charles McKinley), the definition of development goals (Charles Leven), the measurement and evaluation of development (John Krutilla, and Edgar Hoover and Benjamin Chinitz), and a review of

national strategies for regional development (Albert Hirschman, Louis Lefeber, M. A. Rahman, and Hollis B. Chenery).

With such a voluminous task as the editors have set for themselves, there are of course some significant omissions. The volume is admittedly "silent, for instance, on questions of analytical method," and no systematic reference is made to the wide variety of analytical techniques available. The reviewer was pleased to find Walter Isard's "Regional Economic Planning" (Paris, 1961), which has particular relevance to the topic, as well as his "Methods of Regional Analysis" (Cambridge, 1960) at least among the literature cited in part 5.

Although the editorial introductions to the book and to each of its parts endeavor to portray regional development and planning as an integrated whole, the book remains somewhat of a disjointed agglomeration. The selections themselves serve primarily as introductions to the several individual topics. Students of economic geography, regional science, economic development, and regional planning will all find selections from the several fields that are pertinent to their own interest.

H. Albert Green

Essays in Southern Economic Development

Edited by Melvin L. Greenhut and W. Tate Whitman. University of North Carolina Press, Chapel Hill. 498 pages. 1964. $7.50

FOURTEEN PAPERS, which grew out of research supported by the Inter-University Committee for Economic Research on the South through a Ford Foundation grant, are presented in this volume. The editors believe these papers are representative of this research, as well as of great value to scholars interested in a region's economic development.

The book is divided into three untitled parts, each including papers which used common methods of analysis or were concerned with somewhat related themes. Each part has an introductory summary. The papers are outgrowths of the individual interests of the 17 authors. In keeping with this individuality, the editors encouraged each writer to use whatever style he most preferred. The definition of the South varies, but most commonly includes the following 13 States: Alabama, Arkansas, Florida, Georgia, Kentucky, Louisiana, Mississippi, North Carolina, South Carolina, Tennessee, Texas, Virginia, West Virginia.

Apart from general papers, topics treated include the entrepreneurial function, Negro entrepreneurship, "liquidity preference" in Southern banking, population, migration, employment, capital, income and interregional flows, subsidies and various public programs. Some papers stress methodology, particularly factor analysis.

Because of the eclectic approach of this book, the review comments must be quite selective.

During 1950-60, the South's agricultural employment declined 6.29 percent per year, compared to 4.82 percent for the Nation. The South experienced more rapid nonagricultural employment growth than the Nation. Its rates were above the national rates for seven of the eight major nonfarm industry divisions. Yet, the South has remained an essentially rural region with the lowest national rate of urbanization. In 1960, the South still received 10 percent of its total personal income from farming and mining. All the Southern States had per capita incomes below the national average.

From 1930 to 1960, the rate of population increase in the South exceeded the rate of employment increase by 7 percent. In the rest of the Nation, the rate of increase in employment exceeded the rate of increase in population by 11 percent. Danhof and others point to (1) the need for more nonfarm industry to increase per capita incomes in the South, (2) the need to upgrade the skills of the labor force, and (3) the need to develop towns that are good places to live in.

The wealth of reference material should prove invaluable to the serious student of the South. Followup research to guide area development might well focus on smaller geographic areas, again analyzing both rural and urban problems and their interrelationships. Further analysis of contrasting development patterns within the South could be fruitful.

Alan R. Bird

Adjustments and Economic Planning in Canadian Agriculture

By Peter Harsany. Academic Publishing Company, Montreal. 116 pages. 1964. $3.50.

IN RECENT YEARS, increasing attention has been given to forecasts of future developments in Canadian agriculture. A 1957 study, "Progress and Prospects of Canadian Agriculture," by Drummond and Mackenzie, investigated potential changes in demand, technology, and structure of the industry through 1980. MacFarlane and Black developed supply and demand projections for agriculture in their 1958 study, "The Development of Canadian Agriculture to 1970." Agricultural problems were also considered in a recent review by the Economic Council of Canada entitled "Economic Goals for Canada to 1970."

Dr. Harsany draws upon the early Canadian studies and other sources to examine the structure of agriculture and its role in the Canadian economy, and to estimate potential changes in domestic and world demand. On the basis of comparisons with the agriculture of other countries, he evaluates problem areas in Canadian agriculture and recommends adjustments to maximize its efficiency and ability to respond to changes in demand.

The study provides an interesting view of problem areas in Canadian agriculture. It emphasizes the low yields and levels of total output which have contributed to low per capita farm income and an excessive movement of productive resources, particularly labor, to other economic sectors. This problem is related to current Government policies which encourage overspecialization of production and reduce incentives to adopt more efficient practices. The dominant role of wheat in use of land and other farm resources is considered a major weakness, due to low productivity and a potential decline in domestic and export demand relative to other crops and livestock products.

This analysis leads to the conclusion that Canadian agriculture operates far below capacity and that fear of overproduction limits effective action to expand output. Strong Government programs, based upon careful plan-

67

ning, are suggested to stimulate the production needed to meet desired national goals. Those programs should consider potential changes in domestic and world demand, encourage more effective use of present resources, and incorporate additional productive lands into the farming system.

Projections to the year 2000 incorporate adjustments considered feasible under such programs. Addition of new land, the utilization of fallow and unimproved land, and increased use of fertilizer are important to a sharp rise projected for farm output. Major adjustments include a 35 percent reduction in wheat area and a shift of emphasis to livestock, feed grains, oilseeds, and pulses, as well as more intensive production of food crops.

The analysis and implications of the study are subject to debate and the economic feasibility of projected adjustments may be questioned. Despite its controversial nature and its focus upon Canadian problems, the study touches on basic issues applicable to agricultural policy and development in other countries. It will interest many research workers in these fields.

Howard L. Hall

RFD: The Changing Face of Rural America

By Wayne E. Fuller. Indiana University Press, Bloomington. 361 pages. 1964. $6.95.

THE CAMPAIGN for the inauguration of rural free delivery of mail in the 1890's took place against a background of rural dissatisfaction with the farmers' place in the marketing system and in the life of the Nation. The movement became a political football, sometimes blown out of bounds by the changing winds of local, State, and national politics. It frequently met the opposition of top officials in the Post Office Department, as well as that of rural forces which were not convinced of its feasibility. At the local level, it faced the opposition of fourth-class postmasters and small-town merchants who saw in it a threat to their operations. Moreover, opponents asserted that, in the long run, it would contribute to the decay of small rural towns.

Professor Fuller gives many details of the development of the RFD at the turn of the century and the institution of the parcel post in 1912. He has described the two complementary systems as more than a simple extension of the existing mail system. They played an important part in changing the face of rural America. The RFD bridged distances, bringing the farmer and his family into closer contact with friends and relatives and facilitating the transmission of news of the Nation and the world. Consequently, it promoted ideas of democracy and patriotism. The institution of the parcel post made possible the enlargement of the mail order business. It also promoted interest in direct marketing of the farmers' products, which some felt would eliminate the middlemen. The development of both systems became interrelated and dependent upon the development of good roads. Another basic factor in the movement was the shift from horse-drawn vehicles to the automobile and the truck, with their increased speed of delivery.

While Fuller has described in detail the activities of the Post Office Department in the "Farm to Table and Store to Farm" program in the second decade of this century, he has given little attention to the interest and cooperation of the Department of Agriculture, through the activities of the Office of Markets and the then new extension service. Nevertheless, the author has sketched a convincing picture of the influence of postal history on the changing social and economic life of rural areas that should prove a valuable background study for agricultural economists and sociologists.

Vivian Wiser

The Statesman's Year-Book, 1964-65

Edited by S. H. Steinberg. St. Martin's Press, New York. 1,716 pages. 1964. $10.

ECONOMISTS, as well as statesmen, often need a reference volume which gives recent general statistics and political information for each nation in the world, or even for each State in the United States. This well-known manual, now in its 101st annual edition, is just such a reference.

Selected Recent Research Publications in Agricultural Economics Issued by the U.S. Department of Agriculture and Cooperatively by the State Universities and Colleges [1]

Barnhill, Harold E. RESOURCE REQUIREMENTS ON FARMS FOR SPECIFIED OPERATOR INCOMES. U.S. Dept. Agr., Agr. Econ. Rpt. 5, 55 pp., revised November 1964.

Resource requirements for 29 farms in 25 States to earn returns ranging from $2,500 to $5,500 are shown. The 29 farms were programmed at four levels-- $2,500, $3,500, $4,500, and $5,500--of return to operator for his labor and management, beyond interest on entire operational investment and noncash living items furnished by the farm.

Beale, Calvin L., John C. Hudson, and Vera J. Banks. CHARACTERISTICS OF THE U.S. POPULATION BY FARM AND NONFARM ORIGIN. U.S. Dept. Agr., Agr. Econ. Rpt. 66, 24 pp., December 1964.

In May 1958 there were 25.8 million people in the United States 18 years old and over who had been born on farms. The farm-born comprised nearly a fourth of the total civilian population of that age group. About five-eighths of the farm-born adults were no longer living on farms, and one-sixth of all nonfarm residents were persons of farm origin.

Brown, Sidney E., and Eugene C. Pape, Jr. FRESH GRAPEFRUIT PACKAGED AND LABELED INDIAN RIVER--A SALES TEST. U.S. Dept. Agr., Econ. Res. Serv., ERS-212, 8 pp., January 1965.

Fresh Florida grapefruit packaged in polyethylene bags imprinted with the Indian River label produced higher sales than grapefruit displayed loose in tests conducted in Paterson, N.J., in spring 1964. Displays of grapefruit in unlabeled bags were not as effective as the labeled bags but retail movement was greater than from displays of loose fruit.

Bullock, J. Bruce, and Duane Hacklander. PRICE SPREADS FOR BEEF. U.S. Dept. Agr., Misc. Pub. 992, 24 pp., February 1965.

Presents a description of the trends in price spreads for beef during 1949-63. A discussion of the estimating procedure and interpretation of price spread data is also presented, as well as a discussion of short-run fluctuations about the long-run trend in prices and price spreads. Six examples of individual marketings of cattle from ranch and farm point out that differences

between cost and selling price can vary greatly, yielding different returns for similar services at different times.

Clayton, Larry B. COMPLETELY LAUNDERABLE ALL-WOOL APPAREL: THE POTENTIAL MARKET. U.S. Dept. Agr., Mktg. Res. Rpt. 688, 17 pp., January 1965.

Completely launderable all-wool products could utilize 131 million pounds of wool each year. The report is on the potential market for "WURLANized" wool-- the name of a new shrink-resistance process developed by USDA for all-wool fabrics. To get information on possible demand for such a product, USDA economists interviewed management personnel of retail clothing stores across the Nation.

Corley, Joseph R. AN ANALYSIS OF GRAIN TRANSPORTATION IN THE NORTHWEST. U.S. Dept. Agr., Econ. Res. Serv., ERS-200, 49 pp., December 1964.

Country elevator operators in Idaho, Montana, Oregon, Washington, and Wyoming shipped 290.1 million bushels of grain in 1960-61. Seventy percent was shipped by rail and 30 percent by truck. Truck shipments were 26 percent of total shipments in 1958-59.

Cowhig, James D. CHARACTERISTICS OF SCHOOL DROPOUTS AND HIGH SCHOOL GRADUATES, FARM AND NONFARM, 1960. U.S. Dept. Agr., Agr. Econ. Rpt. 65, 32 pp., December 1964.

More than a fourth of the Nation's youth 16 to 24 years old were school dropouts in 1960. The dropout rate was higher among rural than among urban youngsters. For both farm and nonfarm areas, the dropout rate was higher among the nonwhite than among the white school-age population. Dropout rates were very high for youths enrolled in grades below those normal for their age.

Coyner, Mary S. THE AGRICULTURE AND TRADE OF COSTA RICA. U.S. Dept. Agr., Econ. Res. Serv., 30 pp., ERS-Foreign 102, November 1964.

The United States exported $5.5 million in farm products to Costa Rica in 1963. Nearly half of Costa Rica's agricultural imports came from the United States. They consisted mainly of dairy products, wheat, flour, and canned fruits and vegetables. The report includes details of Costa Rican agriculture and trade since 1951.

[1] State publications may be obtained from the issuing agencies of the respective States.

Dennis, Carleton C. THE FEDERAL DATE MARKET-ING ORDER: ACTIVITIES AND ACCOMPLISH-MENTS. U.S. Dept. Agr., Econ. Res. Serv., ERS-214, 19 pp., February 1965.

Since 1955 the gross returns' to growers of dates in California, where production is concentrated, have been relatively stable because of action taken under the Federal Date Marketing Order. This is in contrast to wide fluctuations in returns during the years following World War II. Domestic production now supplies about half of all dates consumed in the United States.

Dunn, Henry A. COTTON BOLL WEEVIL: ABSTRACTS OF RESEARCH PUBLICATIONS, 1843-1960. U.S. Dept. Agr., Misc. Pub. 985, 194 pp., December 1964.

Provides researchers with a quick reference to accomplishments in research on the cotton boll weevil and related information published prior to 1961. State agricultural experiment station publications, USDA publications, professional journals, and other sources are listed.

Gavett, Earle E. TRUCK CROP PRODUCTION PRACTICES, BERRIEN AND VAN BUREN COUNTIES, MICHIGAN, 1959: LABOR, POWER, AND MATERIALS BY OPERATION. U.S. Dept. Agr., Econ. Res. Serv., ERS-206, 49 pp., January 1965.

Eleventh in a group of publications containing information on labor requirements, production practices, and costs involved in the production of truck crops for fresh market and processing.

Gavett, Earle E. TRUCK CROP PRODUCTION PRACTICES, ERIE COUNTY, NEW YORK: LABOR, POWER, AND MATERIALS, BY OPERATION. U.S. Dept. Agr., Econ. Res. Serv., ERS-207, 58 pp., February 1965.

Twelfth in a group of publications containing information on labor requirements, production practices, and costs involved in the production of truck crops for fresh market and processing.

Gertel, Karl. ECONOMIC POTENTIALS OF IRRI-GATION IN NORTH CAROLINA. U.S. Dept. Agr., Econ. Res. Serv., ERS-187, 36 pp., December 1964.

Soils of the Coastal Plain and Piedmont of North Carolina are placed into three major irrigation classes according to likelihood of profitable irrigation. Procedures are also described for adapting the general classification, based on all major crops for which the soil is suited, to a specialized class for tobacco. The classifications will be helpful in estimating yield, water use, and costs of irrigation.

Green, Bernal L. SUMMARIES OF SELECTED PUBLI-CATIONS ON RURAL OUTDOOR RECREATION. U.S. Dept. Agr., Econ. Res. Serv., ERS-190, 25 pp., November 1964.

The report summarizes works dealing with theoretical analysis of recreation, discussion of various outdoor recreational enterprises, and economics of recreation enterprises. It also cites references that provide statistical data on various outdoor recreational activities.

Heady, Earl O., and Walter R. Butcher. EFFECT OF FEED-GRAIN OUTPUT CONTROLS ON RESOURCE USES AND VALUES IN NORTHERN AND SOUTHERN IOWA. Agr. and Home Econ. Expt. Sta., Iowa State Univ., Res. Bul. 531, 34 pp., January 1965.

Efforts to increase farmers' incomes through supported product prices create a need for measures to control production and prevent the accumulation of surplus stocks. This study is concerned with direct control over the output of feed concentrates. The analysis showed that decreased output would lead to increases in the output of substitute products, which could have price-depressing effects on the concentrate crops studied.

Howell, L. D. THE AMERICAN TEXTILE INDUSTRY--COMPETITION, STRUCTURE, FACILITIES, COSTS. U.S. Dept. Agr., Agr. Econ. Rpt. 58, 146 pp., November 1964.

Cotton and wool produced in the United States are confronted with increasing competition from foreign-grown cotton and wool and from manmade fibers. Trends in the nature and extent of this competition are described in the report. Data are presented on changes in supplies, prices, and consumption of American cotton and wool, foreign-grown cotton and wool, and manmade fibers; and on prospects and problems.

LaFerney, Preston E., Robert A. Mullikin, and Walter E. Chapman. EFFECTS OF DEFOLIATION, HAR-VESTING, AND GINNING PRACTICES ON MICRO-NAIRE READING, FIBER PROPERTIES, MANU-FACTURING PERFORMANCE, AND PRODUCT QUALITY OF EL PASO AREA COTTON, SEASON 1960-61. U.S. Dept. Agr., Mktg. Res. Rpt. 690, 32 pp., January 1965.

Sixty-nine bales of Acala 1517C variety cotton were tested. Cotton samples from the field and from the gin were checked in the laboratory to determine the micronaire readings as affected by defoliation treatments. From the producers' standpoint, the most profitable field and ginning conditions were normal defoliation, normal moisture, and minimum cleaning. From the spinners' standpoint, however, the best field and ginning conditions were no defoliation, normal moisture, and minimum cleaning.

Lasley, Floyd A. COORDINATING FLUID MILK SUPPLIES IN THE OKLAHOMA METROPOLITAN MILK MARKET. U.S. Dept. Agr., Mktg. Res. Rpt. 686, 56 pp., November 1964.

Because supply of and demand for milk both fluctuate widely, and often in opposite directions, milk handlers have found it necessary to provide a high degree of flexibility at considerable cost. This study of the Oklahoma Metropolitan Milk Market shows that centralized supply management can decrease both the actual handling cost and the reserve required to meet market needs. Central facilities to process the excess milk from six representative Oklahoma handlers could be operated at less than half the cost of operating individual facilities. Expanding this comparison to all handlers in the market gives an annual cost difference of about $400,000 for processing milk into manufactured products.

Metzler, William H. FARM MECHANIZATION AND LABOR STABILIZATION. Calif. Agr. Expt. Sta., Giannini Found. Rpt. 280, 58 pp., January 1965. (Econ. Res. Serv. cooperating.)

Second in a projected series of three reports on the impact of technological change upon demand for farm labor. The study is centered in Kern County, Calif., one of the Nation's most productive farm areas.

Mills, Theodora. BULGARIA: FOREIGN AGRICULTURAL TRADE. U.S. Dept. Agr., Econ. Res. Serv., 9 pp., ERS-Foreign 104, November 1964.

Despite increasing industrialization, Bulgaria is still primarily an agricultural country. Its agricultural trade, both export and import, is expanding. Bulgaria has become a wheat importing country, and is importing an increasing amount of cotton.

Moe, Lyle E. NIGERIA: PROJECTED LEVEL OF DEMAND, SUPPLY, AND IMPORTS OF FARM PRODUCTS IN 1965 and 1975, WITH IMPLICATIONS FOR U.S. AGRICULTURE. U.S. Dept. Agr., Econ. Res. Serv., ERS-Foreign 105, 15 pp., December 1964.

U.S. wheat exports to Nigeria are projected to reach, at a minimum, 2.2 million bushels in 1965 and 4.2 million bushels by 1975. The United States may also export about 2.8 million pounds of unmanufactured tobacco to Nigeria in 1965 and 1975, and 3,100 metric tons of powdered milk in 1975. The United States may expect to supply at least 67 percent of Nigeria's wheat and tobacco needs in 1965 and 1975 and at least 20 percent of its dry milk needs in 1975.

Pederson, John R., and Fred L. Faber. MAJOR MARKETING CHANNELS FOR SHELL EGGS IN 18 METROPOLITAN AREAS. U.S. Dept. Agr., Econ. Res. Serv., ERS-219, 31 pp., February 1965.

During the study period (1958-61), the predominant marketing channel for the 18 metropolitan areas was from producers to country assembly-shippers to wholesale and producer-distributors, and to food chain stores and independent retailers. Information on volume of eggs handled and marketing functions performed was obtained through mail surveys of all firms thought to be handling 200 or more cases of eggs per month.

Poats, Frederick J., and John W. Thompson. ALTERNATIVE MARKETS FOR CATTLE HIDE TRIM. U.S. Dept. Agr., Econ. Res. Serv., ERS-217, 8 pp., February 1965.

Returns to packers for cattle hides can be greater when shanks, bellies, and heads are removed prior to curing. Fresh hide trimmings have a value of about 2 cents a pound if they are converted into edible collagen, or rendered into feed and oil by a new process.

Thompson, John W., and Frederick J. Poats. ECONOMICS OF SEGMENTING CATTLE HIDES. U.S. Dept. Agr., Econ. Res. Serv., ERS-215, 18 pp., February 1965.

Describes a new hide trimming method which removes the belly and head before curing, and thus reduces curing charges. The new trim removes a little more of the hide than the conventional trim, but increases in yield, weight, quality, and tanning efficiency are large enough to compensate for the cost of the portions removed.

Ulrey, Ivon W. FRESH POTATO TRANSPORTATION TO LARGE MARKETS FROM FIVE MAJOR PRODUCING AREAS. U.S. Dept. Agr., Mktg. Res. Rpt. 687, 31 pp., November 1964.

The report covers major production sources for fresh potatoes in California, Idaho, Maine, New York, and North Dakota-Minnesota. The study emphasizes differences in modes of transporting potatoes to their principal markets and the importance of nearness of production areas to population centers. Potatoes generally are shipped to nearby markets by truck, but by rail to markets farther away.

Vermeer, James, and Ronald O. Aines. THE PILOT CROPLAND CONVERSION PROGRAM: ACCOMPLISHMENTS IN ITS FIRST YEAR, 1963. U.S. Dept. Agr., Agr. Econ. Rpt. 64, 47 pp., November 1964.

The first year of the program helped participating farmers in five areas studied to convert between 12 and 34 percent of their cropland to conservation uses. Most of the land under agreements will remain in the program for 5 years. Payments for conversion ranged from $8 an acre for the poorest land in the program in North Dakota to $70 an acre for the best land in the program in Iowa.

Waldorf, William H. DEMAND FOR MANUFACTURED FOODS, MANUFACTURERS' SERVICES, AND FARM PRODUCTS IN FOOD MANUFACTURING: A STATISTICAL ANALYSIS. U.S. Dept. Agr., Tech. Bul. 1317, 60 pp., December 1964.

From the end of World War I to the late 1950's, U.S. civilian consumption of manufactured farm foods grew at a substantially faster rate than consumption of all farm food products. The study uses a s i m p l e econometric model to explain the behavior of households contributing to this trend. Of all the variables that might have shifted the demand curves, real per capita income was the only empirically significant one. The estimated income elasticity for food manufacturers' services was 0.86; for farm food products used in manufacturing, 0.35; and for manufactured food products, 0.57.

Warren, Cline J. THE AGRICULTURAL ECONOMY OF THE UNITED ARAB REPUBLIC (EGYPT). U.S. Dept. Agr., Foreign Agr. Econ. Rpt. 21, 57 pp., November 1964.

Although industrial gains were made in the last decade, the economy of the United Arab Republic remains primarily an agricultural one. Cotton accounts for 70 percent of all export earnings and occupies close to one-fifth of the total acreage planted annually. Other important cash crops are rice and onions. Because the farming area is limited and the population is increasing, the UAR imports larger quantities of agricultural products each year.

Wilmot, Charles A., and David M. Alberson. EFFECTS OF OVERSIZED MOTORS ON POWER COSTS IN GINNING COTTON. U.S. Dept. Agr., Econ. Res. Serv., ERS-203, 28 pp., November 1964.

Many ginners in California, Arizona, New Mexico, and West Texas are using oversized electric motors, which reduce the power factor level in their plants and result in unnecessarily high power costs. These ginners could save as much as 11 cents per bale in power costs by installing motors of the proper size. The report contains charts which ginners can use in determining power requirements in their own plants.

U.S. Department of Agriculture. THE 1965 WORLD AGRICULTURAL SITUATION. Econ. Res. Serv., Foreign Agr. Econ. Rpt. 22, 40 pp., December 1964.

World agricultural production in 1964/65 is expected to increase about 1 percent over the previous year.

This is a smaller gain than in each of the previous 2 years and also less than the growth in world population and economic activity. Farm output per person is expected to fall about 1 percent, but food output per person will remain about the same as last year.

U.S. Department of Agriculture. WATERSHED PROGRAM EVALUATION: HONEY CREEK, IOWA. Econ. Res. Serv. and Soil Conserv. Serv., ERS-204, 29 pp., January 1965.

Annual benefits from an improvement project on Honey Creek Watershed in Iowa averaged $20,260 between 1955 and 1960. Evaluation of benefits was based on savings through the establishment of conservation measures, prevention of gully damage, reduction in sediment and floodwater damage to roads and bridges, intensified use of flood plains, and reduction in floodwater damage to crops.

U.S. Department of Agriculture. STATISTICAL REPORTING SERVICE OF THE U.S. DEPARTMENT OF AGRICULTURE: SCOPE, METHODS. Statis. Rptg. Serv., Misc. Pub. 967, 234 pp., December 1964.

Presents the organization and statistical procedures used by the Statistical Reporting Service in providing current primary data on the main aspects of the agricultural economy of this country. The publication is designed to satisfy the interests of direct users of the data in agriculture, industry, commerce, Government, and education; students, officials, and businessmen from other countries, and the staff of the Service itself, particularly new employees and trainees.

U.S. Department of Agriculture. THE 1965 WESTERN HEMISPHERE AGRICULTURAL SITUATION. Econ. Res. Serv., ERS-Foreign-113, February 1965.

Western Hemisphere agricultural output in 1964/65 is expected to decline significantly from record levels of a year earlier. Production is down in Canada, the United States, and Latin America. However, the region remains the world's major agricultural supplier. Farm exports will probably be at high levels because of large stocks of most commodities.

U.S. Department of Agriculture. THE 1965 WESTERN EUROPE AGRICULTURAL SITUATION. Econ. Res. Serv., ERS-Foreign-114, 87 pp., February 1965.

Western Europe's economic growth continued at a rapid pace in 1964, although inflation and balance of payments remained serious problems. The rate of growth of the real gross national product was 5 percent or more in 11 out of 16 countries. The combined real product of the EEC grew at a rate of about 5.5 percent.

72

"Demand and Price Analysis: Some Examples From Agriculture," by Dr. Frederick V. Waugh, is now available from USDA (Tech. Bul. 1316, 94 pp., November 1964). It will be helpful to many groups of persons, including undergraduate and graduate students, young researchers who are beginning to get practical experience in demand and price analysis, and agricultural outlook workers in the U.S. Department of Agriculture and in the State extension services. Following are some highlights from the bulletin:

The demand for food is quite inelastic, with respect to both price and income. This statistical fact lies at the heart of the farm problem. A small surplus in agriculture depresses prices severely. And farmers usually get only slight benefits from increases in consumer income.

Since World War II, there apparently have been substantial shifts in the demand for meats. The bulletin analyzes the interrelationships of demand for beef, pork, and chickens.

Money flexibility (the percentage change in the marginal utility of money resulting from a 1 percent increase in income) is estimated by an analysis of food prices.

The bulletin attempts to measure the long-run domestic demand for cotton, using a form of distributed lag. Elasticity of the long-run demand is estimated at about -1.8. This indicates that a 1 percent increase in cotton prices would eventually result in a drop of 1.8 percent in domestic cotton consumption.

The income from a crop is often affected greatly by the crop's distribution among different places, times, forms, and groups of consumers. The bulletin discusses general principles of distribution. It then shows how these principles apply to the diversion of surplus wheat to exports and the diversion of surplus lemons to processed products.

U.S. DEPARTMENT OF AGRICULTURE
Economic Research Service
Washington, D.C. 20250

- - -

Official Business

Postage and Fees Paid
U.S. Department of Agriculture

AGRICULTURAL ECONOMICS
RESEARCH

Is published quarterly by the Economic
Research Service, U.S. Department of Agriculture. Use of funds for printing this
publication approved by the Director of the
Bureau of the Budget (July 31, 1964).

For sale by the Superintendent of Docu-
ments, U.S. Government Printing Office,
Washington, D.C., 20402. 25 cents a single
copy, $1 a year domestic, $1.25 foreign.